100 PRAYERS
EVERY
CHRISTIAN
SHOULD KNOW

100 PRAYERS EVERY CHRISTIAN SHOULD KNOW

BUILD YOUR FAITH WITH THE PRAYERS THAT SHAPED HISTORY

BETHANYHOUSE

a division of Baker Publishing Group
Minneapolis, Minnesota

© 2021 by Bethany House Publishers

Published by Bethany House Publishers
11400 Hampshire Avenue South
Bloomington, Minnesota 55438
www.bethanyhouse.com

Bethany House Publishers is a division of
Baker Publishing Group, Grand Rapids, Michigan

Printed in the United States of America

Library of Congress Cataloging-in-Publication Data
Title: 100 prayers every Christian should know : build your faith with the prayers that shaped history.
Description: Minneapolis, Minnesota : Bethany House, a division of Baker Publishing Group, [2021] | Includes bibliographical references.
Identifiers: LCCN 2021030752 | ISBN 9780764239724 (casebound) | ISBN 9780764238406 (trade paperback) | ISBN 9781493433742 (ebook)
Subjects: LCSH: Prayers.
Classification: LCC BV245 .A135 2021 | DDC 242/.8—dc23
LC record available at https://lccn.loc.gov/2021030752

Unless otherwise indicated, Scripture quotations are from THE HOLY BIBLE, NEW INTERNATIONAL VERSION®, NIV® Copyright © 1973, 1978, 1984, 2011 by Biblica, Inc.® Used by permission. All rights reserved worldwide.

Scripture quotations labeled ESV are from The Holy Bible, English Standard Version® (ESV®), copyright © 2001 by Crossway, a publishing ministry of Good News Publishers. Used by permission. All rights reserved. ESV Text Edition: 2016

Scripture quotations labeled KJV are from the King James Version of the Bible.

Scripture quotations labeled NLT are taken from the Holy Bible, New Living Translation, copyright © 1996, 2004, 2015 by Tyndale House Foundation. Used by permission of Tyndale House Publishers, Inc., Carol Stream, Illinois 60188. All rights reserved.

Cover design by Dan Pitts

Baker Publishing Group publications use paper produced from sustainable forestry practices and post-consumer waste whenever possible.

21 22 23 24 25 26 27   7 6 5 4 3 2 1

CONTENTS

Contents

INTRODUCTION

The very nature of prayer, words spoken to God, ensures that most of them last only a blink, a moment. Some are spoken in the depths of night by worried parents awake, minds racing for what awaits their children. Some are shouted in praise at moments of triumph and victory. Some are just spoken in amazement or wonder or even fear at the glory of the Almighty. Sometimes congregations read words of prayer together from a screen, but then the next slide comes up and the words have entered silence and the prayer is gone.

But we know God collects them. We know He hears and is presented with our words through His Son, in a tradition echoing back through the generations.

But the words themselves—so many of them have vanished, which makes the ones that have lasted through the generations all the more critical.

This book is an effort to collect some of the words that have remained. It is also designed to introduce—or reintroduce—you to some of the men and women who have spoken those words throughout history, because the hearts of believers today and millennia ago beat astoundingly the same.

A great cloud of witnesses.

When the writer of Hebrews sought to encourage members of the early Church, he reminded them of the lives of faith of those who went before. Men and women whose godly lives were captured in the Bible. Abraham and Isaac and Moses and David and Solomon and another and another. Drawing on hundreds of years of history and innumerable stories of faith, the writer creates an image of countless lives before us that point the way to God and serve as examples.

Since then, hundreds of years have passed, and more and more lives have been added to the great cloud. Writers and pastors and missionaries and politicians and mothers and fathers and artists and simple men and women. As we run the race given to us, it's natural, then, to turn to these lives in the same way the writer of Hebrews urged. Not as perfect examples of unblemished faith, for there is no such thing outside of Jesus himself. Instead, for encouragement that, in word and deed, others have run the race before us, and the path is not one we need tread alone.

Perhaps no area of faith is as personal or instructive as prayer. The chance to speak directly to God, to present prayers and petitions to our Lord and Creator, is a sacred opportunity, a holy obligation. But sometimes the words we want to say feel inadequate or like something we've said a million times before. There are lessons we can learn in prayer, too, from those who have come before.

This is a book of some of the most famous and world-changing prayers in history, though we admit to being a little generous with the definition of the word *prayer*. You'll find a few hymns and a few poems in here. Some articles of faith from the history of the Church. All, however, are directed to God and offer a glimpse at the span of Church history and the concerns of the hearts of those who've lifted their voices and thoughts.

Some of the selections you will know and will have read before. What is something new you can find in the words, today, as you perhaps look at them in a new context, a new light? How can new breath be breathed into the familiar?

Others you may have never heard before, but you know of the person who offered it before God. What new facets can these words open in your understanding of that person, and perhaps of a particular time and place? How can the heart of someone one hundred or even two hundred years ago be made to seem relevant and alive today?

Some of the prayers and witnesses will be completely new. We hope a phrase or confession or plea will resonate with your soul. As you dwell on them, or even offer them as a guided prayer yourself, we hope you feel drawn not only into the presence of the Almighty who loves you, but into the awareness of being one witness of many to His ongoing story of redemption.

PRAYERS
for PEACE
and COMFORT

May God our Father and the Lord Jesus Christ give you grace and peace. All praise to God, the Father of our Lord Jesus Christ. God is our merciful Father and the source of all comfort. He comforts us in all our troubles so that we can comfort others. When they are troubled, we will be able to give them the same comfort God has given us.

2 Corinthians 1:2–4 NLT

1

FANNY CROSBY

Known primarily for her hymn writing, Fanny Crosby added as many pages to church hymnals as nearly anyone who has lived. She is credited with more than eight thousand songs of praise, including stalwart favorites like "Blessed Assurance" and "To God Be the Glory." Crosby, born in 1820, was blind from a very young age and became an avid musician while studying at an institute for blind children. She was also a gifted poet, and her mind seemed perfectly formed to capture fragments of praise in stanza and verse.

> *Come in our midst, O gracious Lord,*
> *Unveil Thy smiling face,*
> *Distil in every waiting heart,*
> *The dew of heavenly grace;*
> *From earthly scenes we turn aside,*
> *On Thee we cast our care;*
> *We worship in Thy holy name;*
> *O! bless this hour of prayer.*
>
> *Come in our midst, O gracious Lord,*
> *Thy promise we believe,*
> *That bids us seek and we shall find,*

Ask and we shall receive;
We gather at Thy mercy seat,
Our only hope is there,
We plead the merits of Thy blood;
O! bless this hour of prayer.

Come in our midst, O gracious Lord,
Eternal King of kings,
And fold the children of the law
Beneath Thy mighty wings;
Support the weak, the mourner cheer,
Help all their cross to bear;
Thou spring of joy, Thou source of life,
O! bless this hour of prayer.

WHY THIS PRAYER?

So often a hymn is a prayer that is sung. The words above, written by Crosby in 1868, have the structure and rhyme of a poem and the soul of a prayer. Personalizing the words, changing the pronouns from plural to singular, reveals a portrait of a person attempting to ready their heart for a time of prayer, and hope for the blessing that can be found there. Our only hope is at God's seat of mercy, and whether we find ourselves there for hours during the day or just minutes, each time is an opportunity we should cherish and find refreshment in.

2

PRAYER *of* JABEZ

Tucked into chapter four of 1 Chronicles, Jabez is a man we know little about. We know his mother had such a difficult birth that his name bears that weight. Jabez is a man of sorrow and pain and seems to feel them like a blade hanging over him, because when he calls out to God, a life free from pain is among the things he begs for. He has known his share and wants no more.

Oh, that you would bless me and enlarge my territory! Let your hand be with me, and keep me from harm so that I will be free from pain.

───── WHY THIS PRAYER? ─────

There are surprisingly few verbatim prayers recorded in Scripture. The word *prayer* appears countless times, but usually the prayers themselves are not within quotation marks so we know what the men and women actually prayed. One good reason for this is that most prayers are deeply personal. They're part of a singular conversation—and how often would you want your side of a private, emotional conversation shared? When they do appear in the Bible, then, it must be because there is universal relevance in the words. Jabez's words mirror our own. They can't be the *only* words we offer because they're so focused on ourselves—"bless *me*," "enlarge *my* territory," "keep *me* from harm"—but they're honest in seeking the things we all want from God.

3

THOMAS À KEMPIS

Born Thomas Hemerken around 1380 in Germany, the theologian and writer we know better as Thomas à Kempis is recognized today mostly for his masterwork, *The Imitation of Christ*. He took Holy Orders as a monk in 1413 and became a subprior for the Mount St. Agnes monastery, where he was a scribe and writer. Besides copying the Bible at least four times, Thomas was charged with the instruction of novices, and his writings with that aim were collected to become *The Imitation of Christ*. His premise—that our lives and actions should reflect that of the life of Jesus. The book continues to be in print today and is a key work in world and church literature.

> *Above all things and in all things, O my soul, rest always in God, for He is the everlasting rest of the saints.*
>
> *Grant, most sweet and loving Jesus, that I may seek my repose in You above every creature; above all health and beauty; above every honor and glory; every power and dignity; above all knowledge and cleverness, all riches and arts, all joy and gladness; above all fame and praise, all sweetness and consolation; above every hope and promise, every merit and desire; above all the gifts and favors that You can give or pour down upon me; above all the joy and exultation that the mind*

can receive and feel; and finally, above the angels and archangels and all the heavenly host; above all things visible and invisible; and may I seek my repose in You above everything that is not You, my God.

For You, O Lord my God, are above all things the best. You alone are most high, You alone most powerful. You alone are most sufficient and most satisfying, You alone most sweet and consoling. You alone are most beautiful and loving, You alone most noble and glorious above all things. In You is every perfection that has been or ever will be. Therefore, whatever You give me besides Yourself, whatever You reveal to me concerning Yourself, and whatever You promise, is too small and insufficient when I do not see and fully enjoy You alone. For my heart cannot rest or be fully content until, rising above all gifts and every created thing, it rests in You.

WHY THIS PRAYER?

The list of things we sometimes value more than God is virtually endless, though Thomas à Kempis takes a pretty good stab at it. The fact that he was writing in the fifteenth century—hundreds of years before most of the *things* in the world were even created—should both comfort us and concern us. It is part of human nature to struggle with this. If holy saints have struggled to put God first when their whole life was literally given over to Him, then this is not just a problem that waits in our hearts. At the same time, we have spent the last few hundred years of humanity making it easier and easier to not rely on God. We have gotten healthier, more comfortable, learned more, and become almost as little gods. We need to remember our brokenness and our reliance on God. For our hearts "cannot rest or be fully content until, rising above all gifts and every created thing," they rest in Him.

4

GEORGE WEBB

Our spiritual lives in the West are easy. Though there may be growing concern about the future of faith, right now the freedoms ensconced in the Constitution continue to protect us and our practices. We worship freely, publicly. Verses about the trials that we might face as believers sometimes feel very far away. It's hard to imagine, sometimes, the lives of people who faced persecution again and again. Who fled across an ocean for the chance to practice their faith. The Pilgrims and other early settlers in America came for any number of reasons, but the chance to worship as God called them was high on the list. It meant more than we will ever truly know, and our prayers should be lifted with gratitude for what their hard-fought lives won.

O Lord our God and heavenly Father, which of Thy unspeakable mercy towards us, hast provided meate and drinke for the nourishment of our weake bodies. Grant us peace to use them reverently, as from Thy hands, with thankful hearts: let Thy blessing rest upon these Thy good creatures, to our comfort and sustentation: and grant we humbly beseech Thee, good Lord, that as we doe hunger and thirst for this food of our bodies, so our soules may earnestly long after the food of eternal life, through Jesus Christ, our Lord and Saviour, Amen.

WHY THIS PRAYER?

This prayer is attributed to a Pilgrim named George Webb about whom nothing else is known. We do know the Pilgrims faced deep hardships during their first years, including a drought in 1623 that was so disruptive William Bradford, governor of Plymouth, set aside a day for thanksgiving and confession that eventually became the inspiration and model for our current Thanksgiving. Webb's prayer for the basic human needs of food and drink may not be instantly relatable to us, though many still struggle with meeting fundamental needs. What's concurrently evident is how quickly and fully the prayer moves to the Bread of Life who feeds our soul. Thinking of this, a need as desperate and lifesaving as a sip of water or morsel of food, can give new perspective on spending time in God's word, in worship, in prayer, in Communion, and any other holy moment we can access. We are restored in those moments, filled and satiated, and given the power and energy to go forward with everything else God would call us to.

5

FRANCIS PAGET

Francis Paget was educated at the University of Oxford. After he was ordained, he became a professor of theology there. He completed a number of theological works, including *The Spirit of Discipline*. Later, he was appointed Bishop of Oxford and served in the position until his death in 1911.

Almighty God, from whom all thoughts of truth and peace proceed; kindle we pray thee, in the hearts of all the true love of peace; and guide with thy pure and peaceable wisdom those who take counsel for the nations of the earth; that in tranquility thy Kingdom may go forward, till the earth be filled with the knowledge of thy love: through Jesus Christ our Lord. Amen.

WHY THIS PRAYER?

Paget's prayer here is interesting because it's not just a generic call for peace, but rather a call for a change in the hearts of people, particularly those in power. A so-called time of peace can still be anything but peaceful. Dictatorships can be at peace, but those who live under the thumb of oppression feel the weight of that every day. A true love for peace, however, is about more than just the absence of strife and war. It means pursuing a tranquility echoing the kingdom of heaven, where there will be our lasting and final peace. We've never found it here on earth, but with each heart that is changed, we could come one step closer.

6

QUEEN
LILIʻUOKALANI

The last queen of Hawaiʻi, Queen Liliʻuokalani was born Lydia Liliʻu Loloku Walania Wewehi Kamakaʻeha in 1838. After two brothers' deaths, she was named the heir apparent, and she took the throne in 1891, the first queen ever to rule Hawaiʻi. She would also be the last royal sovereign, as in 1893 business and US government forces led a coup and later imprisoned the Queen. She would fight for reinstatement as monarch and the return of Hawaiʻi to native control, but her hopes ended with the start of the Spanish-American War and William McKinley's election as president. Hawaiʻi was annexed as a territory in 1898 and made a state in 1959.

> *Your loving mercy*
> *Is as high as Heaven*
> *And your truth*
> *So perfect*
>
> *I live in sorrow*
> *Imprisoned*

You are my light
Your glory, my support

Behold not with malevolence
The sins of man
But forgive
And cleanse

And so, O Lord
Protect us beneath your wings
And let peace be our portion
Now and forever more.

Amen

Why This Prayer?

Queen Liliʻuokalani was educated by missionaries early on and raised in faith as a Christian. This prayer was written by her while in prison, and she would later put it to music. The song is sung weekly at churches in Hawaiʻi, remembering both their faith and their history. Forgiveness is perhaps the idea in the Bible that has the greatest gap between how easy it is to talk about and how hard it is to practice. Yet, over and over throughout history we see examples of great men and women often praying for forgiveness while still imprisoned by those who were their enemies. How much easier should it be for us to forgive the petty frustrations and hurts of our everyday relationships? Too often when we feel wronged, we think we deserve to see God's righteous judgment on those who have wounded us, rather than doing the hard work of humbling ourselves and offering forgiveness. What would our lives, what would the world, look like if we did?

PRAYERS
for GUIDANCE
and LIGHT
in the DARKEST
HOURS

You, LORD, are my lamp;
the LORD turns my darkness into light.

2 Samuel 22:29

7

PRAYER *of*
ST. FRANCIS *of* ASSISI

Born Giovanni di Pietro di Bernardone in the early 1180s, St. Francis of Assisi was an Italian friar who almost certainly did not write the words of the prayer that has come to be known by his name. It first appeared, without attribution, in 1912 and eventually went the early twentieth-century version of "viral" by being passed around in various forms attributed to St. Francis. He lived a life that so embodied the prayer that when the words found the page—and become attributed to him—it all seemed too right to be wrong.

> *Lord, make me an instrument of your peace:*
> *where there is hatred, let me sow love;*
> *where there is injury, pardon;*
> *where there is doubt, faith;*
> *where there is despair, hope;*
> *where there is darkness, light;*
> *where there is sadness, joy.*
>
> *O divine Master, grant that I may not so much seek*
> *to be consoled as to console,*

to be understood as to understand,
to be loved as to love.
For it is in giving that we receive,
it is in pardoning that we are pardoned,
and it is in dying that we are born to eternal life.
Amen.

WHY THIS PRAYER?

Chances are, if you read this prayer you may hear a melody come into your mind. Though there are a handful of versions, the most popular was penned in 1967 by Sebastian Temple. Much about the poem seems to resonate with war protests of the late 1960s, so it's not surprising that it found expression at that time. But the words, when you dwell on them, illuminate some of the trickiest paradoxes of the Christian faith—giving to receive, pardoning to be forgiven, and of course dying to receive eternal life. That *death* of our old self is the best way to become a sower of peace—and to find peace all at the same time.

8

WILLIAM
WILBERFORCE

Wilberforce, born in 1759, was a noted and staunch abolitionist in England in the nineteenth century as well as a member of Parliament. All of his hard work advocating for the end of slavery was driven by his faith, and it culminated in the Slavery Abolition Act of 1833. Wilberforce died just days after its passing.

> *O Lord, reassure me with Your quickening Spirit; without You*
> *I can do nothing.*
> *Mortify in me all ambition, vanity, vainglory, worldliness,*
> *pride, selfishness, and resistance from God, and fill me with*
> *love, peace and all the fruits of the Spirit.*
> *O Lord, I know not what I am, but to You I flee for refuge.*
> *I would surrender myself to You, trusting Your precious*
> *promises and against hope believing in hope.*

WHY THIS PRAYER?

One reassuring side effect of reading prayer after prayer by titans of the faith is seeing all of their doubts and pains and questions. God does not demand the lives of saints from all of His believers—rather He compels us to that same spirit of contrition. If these titans are notable for anything it's for *how* much they rely on God. "I know not what I am!" cries a man we still learn about almost three hundred years after his birth. Wilberforce fled to God for refuge, and we must as well.

9

THOMAS DORSEY

Thomas Dorsey grew up in rural Georgia, where his family were sharecroppers. His father was also a local preacher, his mother played music at the church, and the family had an organ at home. Dorsey's early life was filled with church music, but in learning the organ and piano, he soon became steeped in spirituals and the blues. He moved to Chicago to make his living and soon began writing and composing his own works. Only after a spiritual reawakening did he begin working on the songs that would forge his career as one of the greatest gospel songwriters ever. In the end, he wrote more than one thousand songs, including classics like "Precious Lord, Take My Hand," "If You See My Savior," and "Peace in the Valley."

> *Precious Lord, take my hand*
> *Lead me on, let me stand*
> *I'm tired, I'm weak, I'm lone*
> *Through the storm, through the night*
> *Lead me on to the light*
> *Take my hand precious Lord, lead me home*
>
> *When my way grows drear precious Lord linger near*
> *When my light is almost gone*

Hear my cry, hear my call
Hold my hand lest I fall
Take my hand precious Lord, lead me home

When the darkness appears and the night draws near
And the day is past and gone
At the river I stand
Guide my feet, hold my hand
Take my hand precious Lord, lead me home

―――――――――― WHY THIS PRAYER? ――――――――――

Gospel music is a particular amalgam of the blues and spirituals and church hymns, and Dorsey is one of the leading voices in the genre. Beyond being a unique place to give voice to African Americans' faith, the music is important for putting words not just to praise but to the hard times of life. Like the book of Lamentations or the Psalms of lament, there is a time and place for crying out to God in our need and despair. "Through the storm, through the night" Dorsey writes, and those words can stand in for any number of difficulties we might face. Yet there is always God, who is reaching out to us, always a hand ready to take ours and keep us from falling.

10

JONAH

Here's what we know about Jonah, in descending order of popular trivia: Jonah got swallowed by a giant fish or whale. Jonah was a prophet of God. Jonah lived for three dark days inside the animal and then got vomited out. Jonah disobeyed God, ignoring the Lord's call for him to witness to the people of Nineveh. Jonah tried to hide from God by sailing to Tarshish, but he was found by a storm and everyone else on the boat threw him overboard lest they be destroyed also. Jonah called the Ninevites to repentance and then was bitter when their hearts were softened and they turned to the Lord. Jonah sat under a plant God provided for shade and felt he deserved it and then complained when the plant died the next day. Jonah's story lasts only four chapters in the Bible.

> *In my distress I called to the LORD, and he answered me.*
> *From deep in the realm of the dead I called for help, and you*
> *   listened to my cry.*
> *You hurled me into the depths, into the very heart of the seas,*
> *   and the currents swirled about me;*
> *all your waves and breakers swept over me.*

I said, "I have been banished from your sight; yet I will look
  again toward your holy temple."
The engulfing waters threatened me, the deep surrounded me;
  seaweed was wrapped around my head.
To the roots of the mountains I sank down; the earth beneath
  barred me in forever.
But you, LORD my God, brought my life up from the pit.
When my life was ebbing away, I remembered you, LORD, and
  my prayer rose to you, to your holy temple.
Those who cling to worthless idols turn away from God's love
  for them.
But I, with shouts of grateful praise, will sacrifice to you.
What I have vowed I will make good. I will say, "Salvation
  comes from the LORD."

——————— WHY THIS PRAYER? ———————

Why was Jonah chosen as a prophet? We'll never know, of course,
this side of heaven. But in the short glimpse we get into his life,
he did almost nothing "right," and when he did follow God,
it was usually somewhat begrudgingly. About the only time he
modeled a faith worth following was inside the fish. Left without
options, he cried out to God and God listened. Jonah ran away
and pushed God away and tried to forget and yet God's relentless
pursuit of the prophet never ceased. Ninevah was saved—and yet
you wonder if it's really Jonah whom God is trying to capture
and win throughout the book. He chases all of us, and while
we're most likely to turn to Him in our days of darkness, He's
waiting for us wherever we'll meet Him.

11

St. Teresa *of* Ávila

That St. Teresa of Ávila could live as complicated a life as she did from the convent in Ávila, Spain, is proof that all of us—saint and sinner, often in the same person—are unique individuals with lives that are deeply rich and varied. Sometimes the lives of holy men and women in the past seem too focused, too blessed by God to be relatable to those of us who struggle. St. Teresa of Ávila's life and faith are almost impossible to boil down to a sentence or two. Born into a noble family, she was a troublemaker who was sent to a convent as a last resort. She faced illness and periods of separation from God and moments of almost fame for her dynamic personality. She's known for a number of autobiographical spiritual writings, including *The Interior Castle* and *The Way of Perfection*.

> *Let nothing disturb you,*
> *Let nothing frighten you,*
> *All things pass away:*
> *God never changes.*
> *Patience obtains all things.*
> *He who has God*
> *Finds he lacks nothing;*
> *God alone suffices.*

——————— WHY THIS PRAYER? ———————

The difficult thing about a prayer like this is that there are frightening things in the world, there are disturbing things in the world, so being told to ignore them feels like cheap advice. What the prayer offers, however, is the perspective we need to overcome those anxieties. First, so many things that may frighten us are temporary. Our worries are often but for a moment, and God is the same now and tomorrow. The other perspective it offers us is that even in the hardest times, the concerns that last months and years, God is big enough to give us everything we need, at all times. He and He alone is sufficient—and as 2 Corinthians 12 teaches us, His power is actually made perfect in our frailty and weakness.

The O ANTIPHONS *of* ADVENT

For those who didn't grow up in the tradition, an antiphon is a short phrase, most often drawn from the Psalms, that is sung or chanted during mass. The O Antiphons have been part of the Church calendar for centuries, incorporated into Evening Prayers the last seven nights of Advent. The words pull on Old Testament prophecy regarding the promised Messiah, and the urgent invitation is clear: Come!

December 17
O Wisdom of our God Most High,
guiding creation with power and love:
come to teach us the path of knowledge!

December 18
O Leader of the House of Israel,
giver of the Law to Moses on Sinai:
come to rescue us with your mighty power!

December 19
O Root of Jesse's stem,
sign of God's love for all his people:
come to save us without delay!

December 20
O Key of David,
opening the gates of God's eternal Kingdom:
come and free the prisoners of darkness!

December 21
O Radiant Dawn,
splendor of eternal light, sun of justice:
come and shine on those who dwell in darkness and in the
*   shadow of death.*

December 22
O King of all nations and keystone of the Church:
come and save man, whom you formed from the dust!

December 23
O Emmanuel, our King and Giver of Law:
come to save us, Lord our God!

WHY THESE PRAYERS?

Teach us. Rescue us. Save us. Free us. Shine your light on us. Save us. Save us.

These pleas echo our basest needs, especially faced with lives far from God. Prisoners to sin, trapped in darkness, and without the wisdom or words to extricate ourselves from the situation. Even after we become believers, it is too easy to slip into old ways of living. We are the blessed ones. We didn't live thousands of years ago, during the waiting. Those prophetic pleas have been fulfilled through the Wisdom of our God Most High, the Leader of the House of Israel, the Root of Jesse's stem, the Key of David, our Radiant Dawn, our King of all nations, our Emmanuel.

13

Bishop Charles H. Mason

The founder of the Church of God in Christ received no education as a child. His parents were former slaves, then sharecroppers in 1864 Tennessee, and it was their religious upbringing of their son that set him on his path. He received his first call to preach in a Baptist church, but as he began preaching holiness and sanctification he was expelled from the denomination and, with Charles Price Jones, founded the first Church of God in Christ in Little Rock, Arkansas. Eventually separating from Jones, Mason moved the ministry to Memphis, where it became one of the largest African American denominations in the country before going global.

> *Father, thou openeth the gates of wonders, making us enjoy*
> *the gift of the Christ, his word standing. When the wicked*
> *comes against us the power of thy word is for us.*
> *Open the gates of thy wisdom for us and rebuke the power of*
> *the wicked against us. In the glory of Thy council we stand.*
> *The Christ of thy word has made us stand.*

*We see the door of thy mystery. Let the poor confess their sins
and see the glory of thy resurrection. Thy goodness and
greatness is among the daughters. Fill these with the fullness
of Christ. Bless us with light and prudence in the power
of the Holy Ghost. The presence of God is with us and the
blood prevails. Anoint us so we will in Thy pity come to
thee.*

Bless those who have died to sin finding in the spirit.
We enjoy saying the Lord gives us the living bread.
Look to God, be faithful to God, and say no more, "I can't."

WHY THIS PRAYER?

Mason's visit to Los Angeles and the Azusa Street Revival
sparked the spiritual conversion that led Mason into Pentecos-
tal theology. He gave this prayer at Azusa, a testament to the
healing of Jesus' blood and the quickening power of the Holy
Spirit. Mason knew of hard times and difficult circumstances,
and yet often his invocation and charge—to his listeners then
and to us today—is to rely, faithfully, on God and to put aside
the defeatist phrase, "I can't." In Him, we can, and in the darkest
hours and hardest times, that encouragement can be like bread
to a starving appetite.

14

CHARLES VAUGHAN

Charles Vaughan was a nineteenth-century theologian and pastor in England. He was vicar in Doncaster and during his leadership trained more than four hundred young men for service in the ministry who collectively became known as "Vaughan's doves." He wrote commentaries and served on a Bible translation committee.

Look in compassion, O heavenly Father, upon this troubled and divided world. Though we cannot trace your footsteps or understand your working, give us grace to trust you with an undoubting faith; and when your own time is come, reveal, O Lord, that new heaven and new earth wherein dwells righteousness, where the Prince of Peace rules, your Son our Savior Jesus Christ.

WHY THIS PRAYER?

The notion of God's timing is in many ways contradictory or paradoxical because, of course, God stands outside of time. Our eternal God sees and knows all times, and so God's timing can often seem much more about how we understand or interpret what's happening around us than God's specific actions. And yet He does work in the lives of all His children, working within the timeline of our lives, and so we fall back on the "grace to trust . . . with an undoubting faith" no matter the outcome of God's timeline.

15

Naval Prayer

The prayers of war are myriad depending on who is offering them. There are the prayers of the generals and those in the lead-up to the fight, asking for God's wisdom and guidance. There are the prayers of the soldiers both before and in the midst of the battle. For safety. For courage. For the strength to do what they know awaits. There are the prayers of innocents sometimes trapped in the midst of the conflict. They pray for the danger, like the worst of storms, to pass over them without harm. And finally, the prayers of loved ones—often far from the battle—praying for the safety of their husbands, daughters, wives, nephews, grandchildren, and friends. They wait, as they have always waited, for word of safety and health, leaving everything to God's hands.

O Eternal God, may the vessels of our Navy be guarded by Thy gracious Providence and care. May they not bear the sword in vain, but as the defense to those who do well. Graciously bless the officers and men of our Navy. May love of country be engraven on their hearts and may their adventurous spirits and severe toils be duly appreciated by a grateful nation. May their lives be precious in Thy sight, and if ever our ships of war should be engaged in battle, grant that their struggles may be only under an enforced necessity for the defense of what is right. Bless all nations and kindreds on the face of the earth and hasten the time when the principles of holy religion shall so prevail that none shall wage war any more for the purpose of aggression, and none shall need it as a means of defense. All of which blessings we ask through the merits of Jesus Christ our Lord. Amen.

WHY THIS PRAYER?

First offered in 1843 in the Philadelphia shipyard over ships being built there, this prayer has been spoken over every battleship commissioned by the US Navy. For some, war is something we only learn about in school, read about in books, and watch in films. For those of us in the United States especially it has often been something half a world away. For others of us who served in any of the armed forces or have loved ones serving now, it is ever with them. Wars and rumors of wars have followed humans through the generations, and though the prayer offers religion as the only way through war to peace . . . it is a sad fact that religion is also at the heart of so many conflicts. We trust a God larger than any battle, though, who sees the whole scale of human struggle.

PRAYERS
of ADORATION
for GOD

Yours, LORD, is the greatness and the power and the glory
and the majesty and the splendor, for everything in heaven
and earth is yours.
Yours, LORD, is the kingdom; you are exalted as head over all.

1 Chronicles 29:11

16

GLORIA

We don't know the names of the authors of this ancient prayer and hymn. Nor the names of any of the heavenly host who first burst into song on the evening of Jesus' birth. Nor even a single name of a single shepherd who first heard the amazing chorus. But the sentiment, the need to burst into praise of God and His amazing plan, has lingered through all of time and comforts us still.

> *Glory to God in the highest,*
> *and peace to God's people on earth.*
>
> *Lord God, heavenly King,*
> *almighty God and Father,*
> *we worship you, we give you thanks;*
> *we praise you for your glory.*
>
> *Lord Jesus Christ, only Son of the Father,*
> *Lord God, Lamb of God,*
> *you take away the sin of the world:*
> *have mercy on us;*
> *you are seated at the right hand of the Father:*
> *receive our prayer.*

For you alone are the Holy One,
you alone are the Lord,
you alone are the Most High,
Jesus Christ,
with the Holy Spirit,
in the glory of God the Father. Amen.

Why This Prayer?

A fixture at Sunday mass, the Gloria prayer starts with the words of the angels but contents itself with nothing less than the impossible—trying to capture the infinite nature of the Trinity in three simple paragraphs. Just as the shepherds must have stared awestruck into the shining heavens as the angels' song swept over them, so does this prayer invite us to look heavenward as we intone, "For you alone are the Holy One, you alone are the Lord, you alone are the Most High. . . ."

17

MAGNIFICAT—
The PRAYER *of* MARY

Two women, both pregnant. One likely quite young, the other, almost uniquely old. They are cousins, and they are gathering for the first time since both are expecting. Both have been called upon by God to play a particular and honored role in His plan for salvation. Mary, the mother of Jesus, does not speak much through the Gospels, but in this song she speaks with Spirit-guided eloquence, and her words have filled the naves and chancels of churches worldwide.

> *My soul proclaims the greatness of the Lord,*
> *my spirit rejoices in God my Savior*
> *for he has looked with favor on his lowly servant.*
> *From this day all generations will call me blessed:*
> *the Almighty has done great things for me,*
> *and holy is his Name.*
> *He has mercy on those who fear him*
> *in every generation.*
> *He has shown the strength of his arm,*
> *he has scattered the proud in their conceit.*

He has cast down the mighty from their thrones,
and has lifted up the lowly.
He has filled the hungry with good things,
and the rich he has sent away empty.
He has come to the help of his servant Israel
for he remembered his promise of mercy,
the promise he made to our fathers,
to Abraham and his children forever.

Why This Prayer?

Drawn from Luke 1, this prayer rings with Old Testament imagery, and why shouldn't it? Mary was a devout Jewish woman and knew her royal lineage as a descendant of King David. She would know, better than most, the prophecies of *Emmanuel* and God's promise of mercy that He made to Israel. A promise many were beginning to think might never be fulfilled—and yet, in Jesus, the child listening in the womb to Mary's song, the prophecy was fulfilled, not only to Abraham and *his* children but to *all* of God's children who would call on Him. We are His servants. We, like Mary, are called blessed. We sing her song because she sang it first.

18

BLAISE PASCAL

A mathematician and philosopher born in 1623 France, Pascal is probably most known among believers for both his thoughts (*Pensées*) and his wager. *Pensées* stands as a highly regarded philosophical treatise and defense of faith that feels very modern despite being written nearly four hundred years ago. His wager was a simple bit of logic that said, "If your choices are between God and atheism, believing in God makes the most sense, because if you're right you gain eternal life and lose nothing if God doesn't exist. But if you choose the opposite . . ."

> *The year of grace 1654,*
> *Monday, 23 November, feast of St. Clement, pope and*
>   *martyr,*
> *and others in the martyrology.*
> *Vigil of St. Chrysogonus, martyr, and others.*
> *From about half past ten at night until about half past*
>   *midnight,*
> *FIRE.*
> *GOD of Abraham, GOD of Isaac, GOD of Jacob*
> *not of the philosophers and of the learned.*

Certitude. Certitude. Feeling. Joy. Peace.
GOD of Jesus Christ.
My God and your God.
Your GOD will be my God.
Forgetfulness of the world and of everything, except GOD.
He is only found by the ways taught in the Gospel.
Grandeur of the human soul.
Righteous Father, the world has not known you, but I have
    known you.
Joy, joy, joy, tears of joy.
I have departed from him:
They have forsaken me, the fount of living water.
My God, will you leave me?
Let me not be separated from him forever.
This is eternal life, that they know you, the one true God,
and the one that you sent,
Jesus Christ.
Jesus Christ.
Jesus Christ.
I left him; I fled him, renounced, crucified.
Let me never be separated from him.
He is only kept securely by the ways taught in the Gospel:
Renunciation, total and sweet.
Complete submission to Jesus Christ and to my director.
Eternally in joy for a day's exercise on the earth.
Not to forget your words. Amen.

Why This Prayer?

This prayer, this memorial, was written by Pascal to commemorate a deeply personal and supernatural encounter with God that would prove foundational to his faith and life. Pascal came away changed and determined never to forget this moment. He penned these words and then sewed the paper into the lining of a coat he often wore so he'd keep the memorial close to him at all times. These aren't the incredibly eloquent thoughts of a man who would pen books of philosophy—they are the almost inexpressible utterings of any of us when faced with the holy. "Joy, joy, joy, tears of joy."

19

Søren Kierkegaard

Søren Kierkegaard's Danish heritage contributed both the ø to his first name and a Hamlet-esque contemplation of human life. Generally viewed as one of the earliest existential philosophers, his worldview was filtered through a deep and abiding belief in God and faith in Jesus' love. He is best known for the treatises *Either/Or*, *Fear and Trembling*, and *The Sickness Unto Death*, among other writings.

> *Father in Heaven! You have loved us first, help us never to forget that You are love so that this sure conviction might triumph in our hearts over the seduction of the world, over the inquietude of the soul, over the anxiety for the future, over the fright of the past, over the distress of the moment. But grant also that this conviction might discipline our soul so that our heart might remain faithful and sincere in the love which we bear to all those whom You have commanded us to love as we love ourselves.*
>
> *You have loved us first, O God, alas! We speak of it in terms of history as if You have only loved us first but a single time, rather than that without ceasing You have loved us first many things and every day and our whole life through. When we wake up in the morning and turn our soul toward You—You are the first—You have loved us*

first; if I rise at dawn and at the same second turn my soul toward You in prayer, You are there ahead of me, You have loved me first. When I withdraw from the distractions of the day and turn my soul toward You, You are the first and thus forever. And yet we always speak ungratefully as if You have loved us first only once.

───────── WHY THIS PRAYER? ─────────

Like many philosophers, Kierkegaard spent an inordinate amount of his time thinking and writing, and his words fill pages upon pages. The prayer above is one of many found in his journals, some of which eventually inspired a moving and dramatic cantata by Samuel Barber. A good deal of Kierkegaard's writings tackled the enormity of God and put traditional aphorisms to the test. "We love because He first loved us" is a common saying, but this prayer shows how inadequate our view of God's love can be. God loved us not only in the past, but His love is present and future as well. His love for us is always first because He is always first, not because His love found a limit.

20

George Herbert

Born in Wales in 1593, Herbert is best known now as one of the leading poets of the seventeenth century, and one whose work was beloved by Emily Dickinson and T. S. Eliot, among many others. His masterwork is *The Temple*, a collection of poems published in 1633. He also wrote *A Priest to the Temple or, The County Parson His Character and Rule of Holy Life* after having been ordained in the priesthood and taking over a parish outside of Salisbury. He died from consumption the year his poems were printed.

> *I cannot ope mine eyes,*
> *But thou art ready there to catch*
> *My morning-soul and sacrifice:*
> *Then we must needs for that day make a match.*
>
> *My God, what is a heart?*
> *Silver, or gold, or precious stone,*
> *Or starre, or rainbow, or a part*
> *Of all these things, or all of them in one?*
>
> *My God, what is a heart?*
> *That thou shouldst it so eye, and wooe,*

Powring upon it all thy art,
As if that thou hadst nothing els to do?

Indeed mans whole estate
Amounts (and richly) to serve thee:
He did not heav'n and earth create,
Yet studies them, not him by whom they be.

Teach me thy love to know;
That this new light, which now I see,
May both the work and workman show:
Then by a sunne-beam I will climbe to thee.

WHY THIS PRAYER?

Called "Mattens"—or matins—this is a morning poem/prayer found in Herbert's work *The Temple* and patterned after the liturgy of the Anglican church in which he served. Unlike other morning prayers, it's less about turning over every moment to come to God but rather a questioning of why God seeks us out anyway. The last stanza echoes an essay by C. S. Lewis, in which he describes a shaft of light sneaking into a toolshed. Outside of the beam, it illuminates everything in the shed, but dare to step into the light and look up, and the toolshed disappears and all that remains is the light. May every ray of morning light let us see both the One we serve and the work He's provided for us.

21

HANNAH

Hannah is a model of persistence in prayer. Year after year, she prayed to become pregnant. Her husband, Elkanah, did not demand it nor berate her for not having children, but for women in that time, it was of such cultural importance that Hannah would not let herself give up hope. We don't know how her prayers changed over the years, but in 1 Samuel, we read of her voicing to God that this wasn't just a selfish request for her own standing. She would dedicate the child to His service, and that faithfulness was honored by God with the birth of her son, Samuel.

> *My heart exults in the LORD;*
> *my horn is exalted in the LORD.*
> *My mouth derides my enemies,*
> *because I rejoice in your salvation.*
> *There is none holy like the LORD:*
> *for there is none besides you;*
> *there is no rock like our God.*
> *Talk no more so very proudly,*
> *let not arrogance come from your mouth;*
> *for the LORD is a God of knowledge,*
> *and by him actions are weighed.*

The bows of the mighty are broken,
but the feeble bind on strength.
Those who were full have hired themselves out for bread,
but those who were hungry have ceased to hunger.
The barren has borne seven,
but she who has many children is forlorn.
The Lord kills and brings to life;
he brings down to Sheol and raises up.
The Lord makes poor and makes rich;
he brings low and he exalts.
He raises up the poor from the dust;
he lifts the needy from the ash heap
to make them sit with princes
and inherit a seat of honor.
For the pillars of the earth are the Lord's,
and on them he has set the world.
He will guard the feet of his faithful ones,
but the wicked shall be cut off in darkness,
for not by might shall a man prevail.
The adversaries of the Lord shall be broken to pieces;
against them he will thunder in heaven.
The Lord will judge the ends of the earth;
he will give strength to his king
and exalt the horn of his anointed.

Why This Prayer?

We don't know all of the words Hannah lifted to God before becoming pregnant, though she was so wrapped up in intense prayer that the priest took her for drunk. We do know the words she lifted in praise to God after dedicating her son Samuel to His service, and they are recorded in 1 Samuel 2. They are a prayer and song of praise, and yet the words are so much larger than just her circumstances. Like Mary's song, they come out of a very specific and individual circumstance and ascribe to God the power and honor that are His. Hannah's words in particular feel weighted with the years she'd spent in prayer. This is an answer to a long wait, and it is a reversal, one of many that she hints at. Our present circumstances never guarantee our future. We can only lean on God at all times.

22

ST. ELIZABETH ANN SETON

In 1975, Elizabeth Ann Seton became the first person born in the United States to be canonized. Saint Elizabeth Seton was born in colonial New York in 1774. She would go on to establish the first Catholic girls' school in the new country, Saint Joseph's Academy and Free School, and also was the founder of the order of the Sisters of Charity of St. Joseph's. Seton did both of these as a widow, after her husband died of tuberculosis.

Adored Lord, increase my faith—perfect it—crown it your own, your choicest, dearest gift, having drawn me from the pit, and borne me to your fold, keep me in your sweet pastures—and lead me to eternal life.

WHY THIS PRAYER?

The prayer Elizabeth Seton recited often to herself became a calming touchpoint in a life that must have felt so unexpected. She was a devoted wife and mother and lived among the upper class in New York before it all fell apart. Her faith, though, was a constant even in turbulent times. Perhaps it was because she came to her faith and calling somewhat later in life, but she never took it for granted or counted her work as complete. She called on God daily to help her refine and perfect that gift which He offers all of us.

23

THOMAS MORE

Born in England in 1478, Thomas More was a practicing law-yer and entered Parliament at the age of twenty-six. In 1529, he became Lord Chancellor and used his post, in part, to fight against the spread of Protestantism and to oppose the En-glish Reformation. In particular, he refused to acknowledge Henry VIII as head of the church, especially as the king sought to annul his marriage to Catherine of Aragon in order to marry Anne Boleyn. More's steadfastness cost him his life; he was tried for treason and executed. More is the author of *Utopia*, and his life was dramatized in Robert Bolt's play *A Man for All Seasons*.

O my sweet Savior Christ, who in Your undeserved love towards mankind so kindly would suffer the painful death of the cross: suffer not me to be cold or lukewarm in love again towards You.

──────── WHY THIS PRAYER? ────────

Given the arc of More's life, it's a little difficult imagining him being lukewarm about anything—he definitely took sides and stayed there no matter the cost. This prayer, though, isn't about one side or the other, it's about loving God with fire and heat. Jesus' love, after all, could be measured in the heat of His blood that was shed. What is the temperature of our love? How can we kindle it higher?

24

ST. FRANCIS *of* ASSISI

Giovanni di Pietro di Bernardone, now known as St. Francis of Assisi, was an Italian friar who formed the Franciscan order of monks in 1209. Tales of Francis consistently show him understanding God through His creation, and he's become the patron saint of ecology and animals for that.

Holy, holy, holy Lord God Almighty,
Who is, and Who was, and Who is to come:
And let us praise and glorify Him forever.

O Lord our God, You are worthy to receive
praise, glory and honor and blessing.
And let us praise and glorify Him forever.

The Lamb Who was slain is worthy to receive
power and divinity, wisdom and strength,
honor and glory and blessing.
And let us praise and glorify Him forever.

Let us bless the Father and the Son with the Holy Spirit:
And let us praise and glorify Him forever.

Bless the Lord, all you works of the Lord.
And let us praise and glorify Him forever.

Sing praise to our God, all you His servants
and you who fear God, the small and the great.
And let us praise and glorify Him forever.

Let the heaven and earth praise Him Who is glorious.
And let us praise and glorify Him forever.

Every creature in heaven, on earth and under the earth;
and in the sea and those which are in it.
And let us praise and glorify Him forever.

Glory to the Father and to the Son and to the Holy Spirit.
And let us praise and glorify Him forever.

As it was in the beginning, is now, and will be forever.
And let us praise and glorify Him forever.

Why This Prayer?

This prayer was offered by St. Francis to lead off the hourly prayers said by the friars throughout the entire day. "Pray without ceasing," Paul writes in 1 Thessalonians 5:17 (ESV), and we don't often stop to think how impossible that is. It can feel like a difficult hill to climb, but if we think of ourselves as a single voice in a chorus of raised voices to God, we begin to realize that prayers and praises *are* being lifted up to Him endlessly. At this moment, somewhere in the world, at least one voice is calling out to Him. And sometimes it's our voice, praising and glorifying Him forever.

25

THOMAS TRAHERNE

In his day, Thomas Traherne was known mostly as a rector of Credenhill, despite not being ordained until 1660, three years after taking the position. He later also took the position of chaplain to Sir Orlando Bridgeman, Lord Keeper, until Traherne's death in 1674. Few of his written works found audiences during his time. Instead, manuscripts were later discovered in the late 1800s and 1900s and were nearly attributed to other authors, until literary sleuthing connected the writing to the late chaplain of the Lord Keeper. Now Traherne is posthumously seen as a major religious poet of the time, and his major works include *Christian Ethicks* and *A Serious and Patheticall Contemplation of the Mercies of God.*

> *O miracle*
> *Of divine goodness!*
> *O fire! O flame of zeal, and love, and joy!*
> *Ev'n for our earthly bodies, hast thou created all things.*
> *{ visible*
> *All things { material*
> *{ sensible*
> *Animals,*

Vegetables,
Minerals,
Bodies celestial,
Bodies terrestrial,
The four elements,
Volatile spirits,
Trees, herbs, and flowers,
The influences of heaven,
Clouds, vapors, wind,
Dew, rain, hail and snow,
Light and darkness, night and day,
The seasons of the year.
Springs, rivers, fountains, oceans,
Gold, silver, and precious stones.
Corn, wine, and oil,
The sun, moon, and stars,
Cities, nations, kingdoms.
And the bodies of men, the greatest treasures of all,
For each other.
What then, O Lord, hast thou intended for our
Souls, who givest to our bodies such glorious things!

Why This Prayer?

Taken from one of Traherne's poems, this celebration of God's creation, unfathomably complex and diverse, gives us words to think about how much God loves us. Think about those you love and the gifts you've given them through your life. Likely you went out of your way to find the perfect item or bake the meal that's just right for them, challenging yourself to be inventive and creative. All for those you love. When we look at the scope of the universe, and the story we tell of creation, it's a gift given to us. We are to manage it—which we've sometimes struggled with—but it was made for us. God has only appeared corporally on earth for an infinitesimally small amount of time in the person of Jesus. Everything was given to us. And, in the end, our bodies are still just of the earth. The human soul, that divine spark, as Traherne points out, is what is truly important . . . so what amazements and wonders will God have in store for eternity?

PRAYERS
for CHANGED HEARTS

Do not conform to the pattern of this world, but be transformed by the renewing of your mind.

Romans 12:2

26

TIMOTHY DWIGHT

Reverend Timothy Dwight may not be a household name, but he stood at the intersection of a number of important and critical roles during the founding of the United States. Dwight, the grandson of Puritan preacher Jonathan Edwards, graduated from Yale at seventeen and then served as chaplain in the Revolutionary army. He became one of the foremost hymn writers of the time, and many of his songs were said to have deeply inspired the troops of the Connecticut Continental Brigade. After the war, he became a minister in Connecticut, and his influence was so strong he was given the nickname "Pope Dwight." In 1795, he returned to Yale University as their eighth president, where he helped establish the departments of chemistry, law, and medicine. He also helped found the Andover Theological Seminary and the American Board of Commissioners for Foreign Missions.

> *Lord of all worlds, incline Thy bounteous ear,*
> *Thy children's voice, in tender mercy, hear;*
> *Bear Thy blest promise, fixed as hills, in mind,*
> *And shed renewing grace on lost mankind.*
>
> *Let Zion's walls before Thee ceaseless stand,*
> *Dear as Thine eye, and graven on Thy hand;*

From earth's far regions Jacob's sons restore,
Oppressed by man, and scourged by Thee no more.

Then shall mankind no more in darkness mourn,
Then happy nations in a day be born;
From east to west Thy glorious name be one,
And one pure worship hail the eternal Son.

Then shall Thy saints exult with joy divine;
Their virtues quicken, and their lives refine;
Heaven o'er the world unfold a brighter day,
And Jesus spread His reign from sea to sea!

Why This Prayer?

Few hymns from the colonial and Revolutionary years have lasted in the church, and Dwight has authored a number of them. "Lord of all worlds," written in 1808, pulls on Old Testament symbols and imagery to give praise to a God big enough for the challenges of a new country. Dwight's words seem focused on assuring us that God is big enough to take on our challenges. He is the "Lord of all worlds," whose name is the same from "east to west" and whose reign stretches "from sea to sea." This is not a God who can be confined to Jerusalem or Rome or England or any nation. He is a God for the world. Though we may feel distressed when we look for help—"I lift up my eyes to the hills. From where does my help come?" says Psalm 121—God's "blest promise" is the same: Our help "comes from the LORD, who made heaven and earth" (Psalm 121:1–2 ESV).

27

DWIGHT L. MOODY

A towering church figure in late 1800s America, Dwight (D. L.) Moody's heart ached with a call to evangelism. Preaching to staggering crowds at evangelistic meetings across the country, Moody reached countless hearts with his concise and powerful presentation of the Gospel. He also established schools, including Moody Bible Institute, that focused on training the next generation in ministry to reach even further into the world.

Our Heavenly Father, we pray thee that thou wilt give us more and more of the compassion of Christ. We read from the very beginning that he was moved with compassion, as this good Samaritan, when he met this poor, wounded and dying man. O God, give us the spirit of the good Samaritan! May we go from this building and hunt up many to-night, and tell them of Christ and heaven. May we go to the homes of the poor drunkards; may we go to the homes and hearts of gamblers, the homes of the fallen, the despised and the outcast, and tell them of Christ and heaven. O Spirit of God! come down upon this assembly, and may the Church of God find out who their neighbors are. And, O God, we pray thee that they may be filled with the Spirit of Christ, and that they may go and tell others the story of the cross. And, O God, we pray thee that hundreds and thousands in this city may be working to win souls to Christ.

—————————WHY THIS PRAYER?—————————

You can imagine if the massive revival meetings Dwight L. Moody preached at happened today, someone would be holding up a phone, recording every moment, freezing in history every word. The fervor back then was enough that transcripts actually still exist for a number of his events, and you can sense from the words above Moody's heart for reaching into a lost and hurting city. And to do that, he begins, requires taking on the compassion of Christ. Jesus' heart ached for the sick and troubled and, if we dare, that ache can be ours as well.

28

ST. ANSELM

St. Anselm of Canterbury, one of many honorifics by which he was known, was a theologian and scholar while serving as Archbishop of Canterbury in eleventh-century England. Originally born in Italy, Anselm had a penetrating mind and incisive thinking, and his writings leaned away from mysticism toward an attempt to join an understanding of the world with a faith that could embrace that understanding.

> *O my God, teach my heart where and how to seek You,*
> *where and how to find You.*
> *You are my God and You are my all and I have never seen You.*
> *You have made me and remade me,*
> *You have bestowed on me all the good things I possess,*
> *Still I do not know You.*
> *I have not yet done that for which I was made.*
> *Teach me to seek You.*
> *I cannot seek You unless You teach me*
> *or find You unless You show Yourself to me.*
> *Let me seek You in my desire,*
> *let me desire You in my seeking.*
> *Let me find You by loving You,*

let me love You when I find You.
Amen

WHY THIS PRAYER?

For one who sought knowledge and embraced logic and reason, it is not surprising that Anselm's prayer is to be *taught*. This holy man's thoughts sound so much like our own—"You are my God and You are my all and I have never seen You." For those who rely on wisdom and understanding, the tension of relying on faith can be hard to reconcile. Anselm seems to approach it in the best way he knows, by asking God to become his instructor, and in taking on that role, God passes on wisdom beyond our understanding and leads us to a love bigger than any we could imagine.

29

HENRY SCOUGAL

Henry Scougal was an ordained minister and also served as professor of divinity at King's College in the University of Aberdeen in Scotland. He is most well-known for *The Life of God in the Soul of Man*, which was originally written as private correspondence and spiritual advice before being published in 1677. George Whitefield and Charles Wesley were among a number of Great Awakening leaders who found inspiration in the lasting work, with Whitefield saying he "never knew what true religion was" before coming across it.

Fill our souls with such a deep sense and full persuasion of those great truths which thou hast revealed in the gospel, as may influence and regulate our whole conversation; and that the life which we henceforth live in the flesh, we may live through faith in the Son of God. O that the infinite perfections of thy blessed nature, and the astonishing expressions of thy goodness and love, may conquer and overpower our hearts, that they may be constantly rising toward thee in flames of the devoutest affection, and enlarging themselves in sincere and cordial love towards all the world, for thy sake . . .

Why This Prayer?

Taken from *The Life of God in the Soul of Man*, Scougal's prayer is aimed at changing our hearts. Change in a human is one of the most difficult things to enact, as we so easily fall back into patterns and habits often engrained at an early age. If real change is to happen, then most often it must come from outside us. Here Scougal calls on God's Word and truth to live in us, moving us to a love for the world that comes from God. Even a splinter of God's love for the world in us is more than we'd be able to muster on our own, and through His eyes we can see the hurting and needy and broken in the world, and serve where He calls.

30

WILLIAM BOOTH

In 1865, together with his wife, Catherine, William Booth founded The Salvation Army, a ministry devoted to helping the destitute on the streets of London. Fueled by his faith and his desire that the group reach out with both physical relief as well as the Gospel, Booth lived out God's command to feed the hungry and clothe the naked. His organization still thrives, with outposts in over ninety countries, as they continue to reach out and serve those most in need.

> *Thou Christ of burning, cleansing flame,*
> *Send the fire!*
> *Thy blood-bought gift today we claim,*
> *Send the fire!*
> *Look down and see this waiting host,*
> *Give us the promised Holy Ghost,*
> *We want another Pentecost,*
> *Send the fire!*
>
> *God of Elijah, hear our cry:*
> *Send the fire!*
> *To make us fit to live or die,*
> *Send the fire!*
> *To burn up every trace of sin,*
> *To bring the light and glory in,*

The revolution now begin,
Send the fire!

'Tis fire we want, for fire we plead,
Send the fire!
The fire will meet our every need,
Send the fire!
For strength to ever do the right,
For grace to conquer in the fight,
For power to walk the world in white,
Send the fire!

To make our weak hearts strong and brave,
Send the fire!
To live a dying world to save,
Send the fire!
O see us on thy altar lay
Our lives, our all, this very day,
To crown the offering now we pray,
Send the fire!

WHY THIS PRAYER?

The Holy Spirit can appear in different forms but perhaps is most recognized as fire from the book of Acts and Pentecost. Fire's uses are almost innumerable, and being able to harness it is what helped humans create societies and reach our current age. Whether keeping us warm in the depths of night or cooking our food or forging the metals and tools so critical to our lives, fire impacts our lives in so many ways. So should the fire of the Holy Spirit impact our spirit. It refines us, lights our path, and gives us God's light inside us that shines like a beacon on a hill. Booth pleads for the Spirit to work in his life, and no matter our denomination or background, we should actively seek to know this burning, wondrous facet of God's nature.

31

BILLY SUNDAY

William A. Sunday is not a made-up name, though few have
been born with a better name for their eventual calling. Born
in 1862, Billy Sunday was no stranger to crowds or the spotlight, first playing major league baseball for the Chicago White
Stockings and Philadelphia Phillies, among others, and later
becoming one of the best-known revival evangelists in the
country. He also became one of the first preachers to take to
radio waves.

> *Now, Lord, I'm not here to have a good time. I am here to show
> what you are doing for these people and to tell them that you are
> willing to save them and to bear their burdens if they will give their
> hearts to you.*
>
> *Well, Jesus, I'm not up in heaven yet. I don't want to go, not yet.
> I know it's an awful pretty place, Lord. I know you'll look after me
> when I get there. But, Jesus, I'd like to stay here a long time yet. I
> don't want to leave Nell and the children. I like the little bungalow
> we have out at the lake. I know you'll have a prettier one up there. If
> you'll let me, Jesus, I'd like to stay here, and I'll work harder for you
> if I can. I know I'll go there, Jesus, and I know there's lots of men and
> women here in this Tabernacle tonight who won't go.*

Solomon found it was all vanity and vexation of spirit. They're living that way today, Jesus. I say that to you here tonight, banker; to you, Commercial Club; to you, men from the stockyards. If you want to live right, choose Jesus as your Saviour, for man's highest happiness is his obedience to Jesus Christ. And now, while we're all still, who'll come down and say "I'm looking above the world?" Solomon said it was all vanity. Why certainly, you poor fool. He knew. But I'm glad you saw the light, Solomon, and spread out your wings.

O Lord, bend over the battlements of glory and hear the cry of old Pittsburgh. O Lord, do you hear us? Lord, save tens of thousands of souls in this old city. Lord, everybody is helping. Lord, they are keeping their churches closed so tight that a burglar couldn't get in with a jimmy. Lord, the angels will shout to glory and the old devil will say, What did they shut up the churches of Pittsburgh for, when they have so many good preachers, and build a Tabernacle and bring a man on here to take the people away from me? O Lord, we'll win this whisky-soaked, vice-ridden old city of Pittsburgh and lay it at your feet and purify it until it is like paraffine.

WHY THIS PRAYER?

In its history, the United States has given rise to a nearly inexhaustible supply of charismatic preachers who have preached the Word of God and become celebrities because of it. Billy Sunday sits high on that list. Two things are true at the same time: Billy Sunday became quite wealthy preaching the Gospel—he mentions his little bungalow on the lake; and, countless men and women came to the Lord through his tabernacle meetings and because of hearing the Gospel on the radio. Sunday could both serve as the model for Sinclair Lewis's satiric *Elmer Gantry* and also earnestly stand in front of what's reckoned to be over 80 million in crowds and preach and pray with all his heart. Pittsburgh is just one city of many he passed through.

It was no more or less sinful than any place, no more or less in need of the word of the Gospel to find those in need. We have different Billy Sundays today, but the simple life-changing message should not change: "If you want to live right, choose Jesus as your Saviour, for man's highest happiness is his obedience to Jesus Christ."

32

FYODOR DOSTOEVSKY

Dostoevsky is one of the titans of Russian literature, having penned *Crime and Punishment*, *The Idiot*, *Notes from Underground*, and *The Brothers Karamazov*. Born in 1821 Moscow, Dostoevsky at one point was sentenced to death because he belonged to a group devoted to discussing books banned by the Tsar. Dostoevsky's works tackle hard questions of human existence while shining a light on spiritual truths he held close, having been raised in the Russian Orthodox church.

Remember, too, every day, and whenever you can, repeat to yourself, "Lord, have mercy on all who appear before Thee today." For every hour and every moment thousands of men leave life on this earth, and their souls appear before God. And how many of them depart in solitude, unknown, sad, dejected that no one mourns for them or even knows whether they have lived or not! And behold, from the other end of the earth perhaps, your prayer for their rest will rise up to God though you knew them not nor they you. How touching it must be to a soul standing in dread before the Lord to feel at that instant that, for him too, there is one to pray, that there is a fellow creature left on earth to love him too! And God will look on you both more graciously, for if you have had so much pity on him, how much more will

*He have pity Who is infinitely more loving and merciful than you!
And He will forgive him for your sake.*

*Brothers, have no fear of men's sin. Love a man even in his sin, for
that is the semblance of Divine Love and is the highest love on earth.
Love all God's creation, the whole and every grain of sand in it. Love
every leaf, every ray of God's light. Love the animals, love the plants,
love everything. If you love everything, you will perceive the divine
mystery in things. Once you perceive it, you will begin to comprehend
it better every day. And you will come at last to love the whole world
with an all-embracing love.*

WHY THIS PRAYER?

Spoken by Father Zossima in *The Brothers Karamazov*, the prayer
and wisdom offered points us to a humble and merciful spirit. It
is easy to put ourselves first in prayer—this is *our* time, after all,
to talk to God and share what's on our heart. But the opportunity
to pray for others is an honor and privilege and delights God. We
all know people whose particular gift is the willingness to take
on the burdens of others in prayer and who keep long lists of
ongoing concerns. To add even a hint of that selflessness to our
prayer life can help us gain perspective on our own troubles as we
see, yet again, that we're part of a large family of believers—and
that God is large enough to care for us all.

33

CHARLES SPURGEON

The "Prince of Preachers," Charles Spurgeon was a nineteenth-century English pastor of London's New Park Street Chapel and Metropolitan Tabernacle whose legacy still looms large over modern Christian faith. Spurgeon's heartbeat for evangelism and his preaching, writing, and widespread speaking won tens of thousands to Jesus. He also founded ministries devoted to caring for the sick and needy.

We would offer a prayer to Thee for those who are quite strange to the work of the Spirit of God, who have never owned their God, who have lived as if there were no God. Open their eyes that they may see God even though that sight should make them tremble and wish to die. O! let none of us live without our God and Father. Take away the heart of stone, take away the frivolities, the levity, the giddiness of our youth, and give us in downright earnest to seek true happiness where alone it can be found, in reconciliation to God, and in conformity to His will.

Lord, save the careless, save the sinful, the drunkard, take away from him his cups. The unholy and unjust men, deliver these from their filthiness. The dishonest and false, renew them in their lives and any that are lovers of pleasure, dead while they live, and any that are lovers of self, whose life is bounded by the narrowness of their own being, the Lord renew them, regenerate them, make them new creatures in Christ Jesus. For this we do fervently pray.

Lord God the Holy Ghost, may faith grow in men. May they believe in Christ to the saving of their souls. May their little faith brighten into strong faith and may their strong faith ripen into the full assurance of faith. May we all have this last blessing. May we believe God fully. May we never waver. Resting in the great Surety and High Priest of the New Covenant may we feel "the peace of God which passeth all understanding," and may we enter into rest.

Why This Prayer?

Given his résumé and the lives he impacted, it's worth looking at how a man like Spurgeon prayed for nonbelievers. First, this is only a section of a much longer prayer, so it's clear he unleashed his passion on behalf of the lost. There are times when concise and narrow thoughts convey exactly the prayer we need and times when the messy tumult of our soul just opens itself to God. Spurgeon looked out on London, a wild and reckless city as almost all are, and saw all stripes and shades of needy. He knew his part, too, that he was a spark that might light a small flame of faith, but that the hard work after that still waited. And that all of us should pray for the same blessing, that our faith would grow from flame to fire, in the assurance and rest of Jesus.

PRAYERS
for JUSTICE
in the FACE
of EVIL

When justice is done, it brings joy to the righteous but terror to evildoers.

Proverbs 21:15

34

Sojourner Truth

Sojourner Truth escaped from slavery to freedom in 1827 and became a powerful activist for abolition, suffrage, and women's rights. Born Isabella Bomfree, she renamed herself Sojourner Truth, one of history's great names, in 1843, compelled by the Holy Spirit to speak a vision for equality, not just for races but gender as well. Her "Ain't I a Woman?" speech at the 1851 Women's Rights Convention continues to be a historical touchpoint in the movement.

Oh, God, make the people hear me—don't let them turn me off, without hearing and helping me.

Why This Prayer?

Put to paper in *The Narrative of Sojourner Truth*, this prayer was spoken during her attempts to claim her enslaved son, after herself gaining freedom. She had escaped with her daughter, but she needed the advocacy of the courts in a lawsuit to gain her son's freedom. That she won is a testament to not only the power of her prayers but the righteousness of her cause. Her prayer is one that fits the rest of her life, as well, as she began to speak and advocate around the country on behalf of those most in need. Sometimes, in times of dire need, what we most need is simply to be heard.

35

HARRIET TUBMAN

Born enslaved in Maryland by the name Araminta Ross, Harriet Tubman eventually escaped and became known as the "Moses of her people" because of her work with the Underground Railroad. She is connected with over a dozen missions to help multiple dozens escape slavery toward freedom. Legend and history have woven around her and her words, but what we can find of the truth of her life needs little embellishment. A spy and scout for the Union army during the Civil War and an activist for women's suffrage, Tubman lived out her alleged quote to just "Keep going," whether she actually said it or not.

"Oh Lord, convert master!" "Oh Lord, change that man's heart!" . . .

"And so," said she, "I prayed all night long for master, till the first of March; and all the time he was bringing people to look at me, and trying to sell me. Then we heard that some of us was going to be sold to go with the chain-gang down to the cotton and rice fields, and they said I was going, and my brothers, and sisters. Then I changed my prayer. First of March I began to pray, 'Oh, Lord, if you [aren't] never going to change that man's heart, kill him, Lord, and take him out of the way.'"

──────────── WHY THIS PRAYER? ────────────

It's an impossibly difficult prayer to read—dark thoughts from terrible times. The words are attributed to Tubman, written in an early biography. What's interesting, though, is to think about her plight in comparison to Moses, with whom she was often linked. How many times did Moses appear before Pharaoh begging him to release the Israelites, knowing the punishment that would be forthcoming? That Harriet would pray the same way should not be a surprise. What she seeks is God's mercy and God's justice. She can only offer her painfully honest words. Prayer isn't the time to self-censor. It's about showing the heart of our joys and pains, and then trusting God with whatever comes next.

36

FREDERICK DOUGLASS

Frederick Douglass was a powerhouse speaker and writer and a galvanizing force for abolition. He was born into slavery in Maryland around February 1818. He chronicled his life in a number of works, including the *Narrative of the Life of Frederick Douglass, an American Slave*, a bestseller upon its publication. He escaped in 1838 and soon set up his new life in Massachusetts, where he became connected with William Lloyd Garrison, publisher of *The Liberator* and one of the key abolitionists of the time. Douglass soon became a critical voice and example in the path to freedom for enslaved peoples.

> *Just God! and these are they,*
> *Who minister at thine altar, God of right!*
> *Men who their hands, with prayer and blessing, lay*
> *On Israel's ark of light.*
>
> *What! preach, and kidnap men?*
> *Give thanks, and rob thy own afflicted poor?*
> *Talk of thy glorious liberty, and then*
> *Bolt hard the captive's door?*

What! servants of thy own
Merciful Son, who came to seek and save
The homeless and the outcast, fettering down
The tasked and plundered slave!

Pilate and Herod friends!
Chief priests and rulers, as of old, combine!
Just God and holy! is that church which lends
Strength to the spoiler thine?

─────────── WHY THIS PRAYER? ───────────

The United States continues to grapple with the terrible legacy of slavery and racial discrimination, though we're more than one hundred and fifty years after the Emancipation Proclamation. Though "we are all one in Christ," churches in the United States are not immune to the same issues dividing our country, and there is a difficult legacy that must be faced. Frederick Douglass had no difficulty playing prophet to the pastors and "good Christians" in slave-holding states who supported the awful institution. It is never a comfortable thing to be linked with Pilate and Herod, yet the church is not automatically in the right. We must be held accountable for all our teachings and actions, and when they stand in opposition to God's directives, we must turn, or face the judgment that will come to us.

37

AMANDA BERRY SMITH

Born into slavery, Amanda Berry Smith eventually led a life that took her into revival tents, across the sea to England and India on mission trips, and then back to the United States, where she founded an orphanage in later life. Gaining emancipation brought a life that would have been impossible under the shackles of slavery. Smith was linked with the Underground Railroad and the NAACP's founding, and she burned for justice to emerge from faith.

Help me to throw off that mean feeling, and give me grace to be a gazing stock.

——— WHY THIS PRAYER? ———

The full title of Smith's autobiography is *An Autobiography: The Story of the Lord's Dealings with Mrs. Amanda Smith, the Colored Evangelist: Containing an Account of Her Life Work of Faith, and Her Travels in America, England, Ireland, Scotland, India, and Africa as an Independent Missionary*. This prayer is pulled from that book, a section recounting Smith's earliest days speaking as an African American woman at what were predominately white tent meetings, where she was looked on with suspicion and curiosity and often hatred. In these most difficult circumstances, she called on God to give her the spirit and heart not just to make it through, but to share His Word and message. Too often, especially in confrontations or difficult circumstances, we are ruled by our tongue. If we can manage to wait a second, to take a moment of prayer, perhaps we can ask for the fresh air of grace to find us as well.

38

W. E. B. Du Bois

In 1903, William Edward Burghardt Du Bois wrote *The Negro Church*, a sociological study of the black church based on interviews with more than one thousand congregants. 1903 was a monumental year for Du Bois, as he also published *The Souls of Black Folk*, which became a cornerstone piece of African American literature, challenging white supremacist notions of black inferiority and even the pervasive nineteenth-century theory that black people had no soul. Instead, Du Bois's book celebrated the vital and vibrant culture at the heart of African American church life and pointed to the Gospel, which offers salvation and equality to all.

Behold this maimed and broken thing; dear God, it was an humble black man who toiled and sweat to save a bit from the pittance paid him. They told him: Work and Rise. He worked. Did this man sin? Nay, but some one told how some one said another did—one whom he had never seen nor known. Yet for that man's crime this man lieth maimed and murdered, his wife naked to shame, his children, to poverty and evil.

Hear us, O Heavenly Father!

Doth not this justice of hell stink in Thy nostrils, O God? How long shall the mounting flood of innocent blood roar in Thine ears and pound in our hearts for vengeance? Pile the pale frenzy of blood-crazed brutes who do such deeds high on Thine altar, Jehovah Jireh, and burn it in hell forever and forever!

Forgive us, good Lord; we know not what we say!

Bewildered we are, and passion-tost, mad with the madness of a mobbed and mocked and murdered people; straining at the armposts of Thy Throne, we raise our shackled hands and charge Thee, God, by the bones of our stolen fathers, by the tears of our dead mothers, by the very blood of Thy crucified Christ: What meaneth this? Tell us the Plan; give us the Sign!

Keep not thou silence, O God!

Sit no longer blind, Lord God, deaf to our prayer and dumb to our dumb suffering. Surely Thou too art not white, O Lord, a pale, bloodless, heartless thing?

Ah! Christ of all the Pities!

Forgive the thought! Forgive these wild, blasphemous words. Thou art still the God of our black fathers, and in Thy soul's soul sit some soft darkenings of the evening, some shadowings of the velvet night.

WHY THIS PRAYER?

What were the prayers of the Israelites during their years in captivity? What were the cries of the early Church as Rome tried to wipe them from the earth? What are the *emotions* of any who feel they pray in righteousness and receive no relief? W. E. B. Du Bois's poem "A Litany of Atlanta" is an emotion-filled poem. It's fueled by the question of how black people, particularly those in the church, should think about God in a country where white Christians persecuted, lynched, and marginalized them. There is a plea for justice and a cry of the soul. It is an eloquent and heartbreaking lament on a divisive topic that continues to haunt this country today.

39

MARIA W. STEWART

Maria W. Stewart stands among the earliest black political voices in US history. Born free in 1803 but orphaned as a young girl, she spent numerous years as an indentured servant before gaining full freedom and moving to Boston. There she married and found a vibrant black community in the Beacon Hill neighborhood. Her husband died only a few years after their marriage, and Maria became more and more involved in both her church and the growing abolitionist movement. In 1831 she published *Religion and the Pure Principles of Morality, the Sure Foundation on Which We Must Build* and wrote for William Lloyd Garrison's abolitionist journal. The publications led to speaking engagements, and she is one of the first recorded women of any race speaking in public.

> *Almighty God, it is the glorious hope of a blessed immortality beyond the grave that supports thy children through this vale of tears. Forever blessed be thy name, that thou hast implanted this hope in my bosom. If thou hast indeed plucked my soul as a brand from the burning, it is not because thou hast seen any worth in me; but it is because of thy distinguishing mercy, for mercy is thy darling attribute, and thou de-lightest in mercy, and art not willing that any should perish, but that*

*all should come to the knowledge of the truth as it is in Jesus. Clothe
my soul with humility as with a garment. Grant that I may bring forth
the fruits of a meek and quiet spirit. Enable me to adorn the doctrines
of God my Saviour by a well-regulated life and conversation. May I
become holy, even as thou art holy, and pure, even as thou art pure.
Bless all my friends and benefactors—those who have given me a
cup of cold water in thy name, the Lord reward them. Forgive all my
enemies. May I love them that hate me, and pray for them that de-
spitefully use and persecute me. Preserve me from slanderous tongues,
O God, and let not my good be evil spoken of. Let not a repining
thought enter my heart, nor a murmuring sigh heave from my bosom;
but may I cheerfully bear with all the trials of life. Clothe me with the
pure robes of Christ's righteousness, and that when he shall come in
flaming fire to judge the world, I may appear before him with joy, and
not with grief; and not only for myself do I ask these blessings, but for
all the sons and daughters of Adam, as thou art no respecter of persons, and as all distinctions wither in the grave. Grant all prejudices
and animosities may cease from among men. May we all realize that
promotion cometh not from the East nor from the West, but that it
is God that putteth up one and setteth down another. May the rich
be rich in faith and good works toward our Lord Jesus Christ, and
may the poor have an inheritance among the saints in light, a crown
incorruptible that fadeth not away, eternal in the heavens. And now
what wait we for? Be pleased to grant that we may at last join with
all the Israel of God in celebrating thy praise.*

Why This Prayer?

Stewart's prayer is comprehensive. It is a prayer for all of life,
built on the structure of the Lord's Prayer. It's a prayer from
which you can take a fragment of what you need for a day . . .
or linger over it and see how it captures all of the life of faith.
We know she spoke and wrote eloquently on issues of race and
the need for equality and justice. And her prayer that "prejudice

and animosities may cease" is certainly a part of what she calls out for. But it's not the only part. She didn't forget to pray for God to move in her own life—to purify her and clothe her with humility—even as she worked on behalf of God's calling. If we believe we are on the side of righteousness, it is easy to be caught up only in that fight, risking becoming blind to our own deficiencies and all the other needs around us.

PRAYERS
for a NATION
to BE MOVED

For in him all things were created: things in heaven and on earth, visible and invisible, whether thrones or powers or rulers or authorities; all things have been created through him and for him.

Colossians 1:15

40

ABRAHAM LINCOLN

For such a giant in United States history, Lincoln's actual political career is shockingly short. He served a single term as US Representative from Illinois from 1847 to 1849. Then he was elected the sixteenth president of the United States in 1860 and reelected in 1864 before his untimely assassination. Six and a half years and yet a legacy as large as any.

> *Fondly do we hope—fervently do we pray—that this mighty scourge of war may speedily pass away. Yet, if God wills that it continue . . . until every drop of blood drawn with the lash, shall be paid by another drawn with the sword . . . so still it must be said "the judgments of the Lord, are true and righteous altogether."*
>
> *With malice toward none; with charity for all; with firmness in the right, as God gives us to see the right, let us strive on to finish the work we are in; to bind up the nation's wounds; to care for him who shall have borne the battle, and for his widow, and his orphan—to do all which may achieve and cherish a just and a lasting peace, among ourselves, and with all nations.*

Why This Prayer?

Technically, it's part of an address or speech, but the words directed to God as a plea for peace certainly read as a prayer. The Civil War had been raging for four years, but an end now seemed to be in sight. Abraham Lincoln, who had led America through its darkest time, now looked at another four years of serving as president, and perhaps the chance to unify a nation torn apart. Speaking into his hope for the future—but not knowing what would come for the country or himself—he leaned on the unchanging nature of God and the assurance of trusting His ways. We know what the weeks and months ahead would deliver for Lincoln, who was brought down by violence, but his pleas for the country to be kept together were answered.

41

GEORGE WASHINGTON

This founding father casts an enormous shadow on US history as general of the Revolutionary forces that prevailed against perhaps the greatest army the world then knew, followed by eight years as the very first president of the newly established United States. To his credit, Washington never sought power. He had to be encouraged to take the office of president and stepped away after two terms despite many wanting him to continue. He believed that the strength of the country, though, rested not in a single man but in its citizens.

I now make it my earnest prayer, that God would have you and the State over which you preside, in his holy protection that he would incline the hearts of the Citizens to cultivate a spirit of subordination and obedience to Government, to entertain a brotherly affection and love for one another, for their fellow Citizens of the United States at large and particularly for their brethren who have served in the field—and finally that he would most graciously be pleas'd to dispose us all to do Justice, to love mercy and to demean ourselves, with that Charity, humility and pacific temper of mind, which were

the Characteristicks of the Devine Author of our blessed Religion and
without an humble immitation of whose example in these things, we
can never hope to be a happy Nation.

Why This Prayer?

Written by Washington in 1783, prior to his becoming president, this prayer includes reference to Micah 6:8 and the prophet's concise recitation of what God requires of all people: that we act justly, love mercy, and walk humbly with Him. The war had been won, but the country now sat in a kind of strange limbo, newly independent and struggling, like a gawky newborn colt or fawn, to find its footing. Washington intended to retire to private life at Mt. Vernon but put to page his best advice for the new country, hoping that the citizens would draw together. We have always been a diverse blend of ideas and notions. At times, we've stretched the very bonds of the country to their limits. Washington's words point to a different path, one that he felt God would truly bless.

42

RONALD REAGAN

Ronald Regan served two terms as president of the United States from 1981 to 1989. A Hollywood actor as a young man, Reagan eventually became governor of California and later the country's fortieth president. He survived an assassination attempt, and his eight years in office coincided with the tense final years of the Cold War with the USSR. A polarizing figure for many now, he linked US party politics to evangelical faith in a way never seen before.

> *Let us, young and old, join together, as did the First Continental Congress, in the first step—humble, heartfelt prayer. Let us do so for the love of God and His great goodness, in search of His guidance and the grace of repentance, in seeking His blessings, His peace, and the resting of His kind and holy hands on ourselves, our Nation, our friends in the defense of freedom, and all mankind, now and always.*

———————— WHY THIS PRAYER? ————————

While National Days of Prayer have been common since the very founding of the nation, the day was not made official until President Harry Truman signed a bill into law in April 1952. Since that time, every sitting president has recognized the day—Republican and Democrat alike. The words above were offered by President Reagan in 1988. Adept at blending faith and history, politics and religion together, Reagan called the US a "shining city on a hill" prior to his first election, hearkening to the words of Matthew 5 to describe believers. There will always be tension between the powers of politics and the path God calls us to, but his call that our first step should be prayer is a model that would serve every one of us well—private and public citizens alike.

43

JOHN JAY

Where Washington, Adams, Jefferson, Franklin, and now even Hamilton have names indelibly recognized in US history as founding fathers, John Jay has slipped under the radar in popular history. His legacy is broad and diverse, however. Jay coauthored the Federalist Papers with Hamilton and Madison, spent time as a diplomat to Spain, was appointed by Washington as the first chief justice of the Supreme Court, and afterward took the role of governor of New York. Though he didn't sign the Declaration of Independence, he did serve as president of the Congressional Congress and his fingerprints are all over the documents that would forge the beginnings of the United States.

> *I thank thee, the great Sovereign of the universe, for thy long-continued goodness to these countries, notwithstanding our ingratitude and disobedience to thee, our merciful deliverer and benefactor. Give us grace to turn unto thee with true repentance, and implore thy forgiveness. And be pleased to forgive us; and bless us with such portions of prosperity as thou seest to be fit for us, and with rulers who fear thee, and walk in the paths which our Saviour hath set before us. Be pleased to bless all nations with the knowledge of thy gospel,—and may thy holy will be done on earth as it is done in heaven.*

Condescend, merciful Father! to grant as far as proper these imperfect petitions, to accept these inadequate thanksgivings, and to pardon whatever of sin hath mingled in them, for the sake of Jesus Christ, our blessed Lord and Saviour; unto whom, with thee, and the blessed Spirit, ever one God, be rendered all honour and glory, now and for ever.

WHY THIS PRAYER?

A portion of a long prayer found among Jay's writings, the selection above reveals the man as one guided by his faith, seeking God's leading not only in personal decisions but for the direction of the nation—and the entire world. Jay's position is one of humility and confession, never assuming we have earned or deserve God's blessing as a country. The heart of a single man or woman is complicated enough—the beating heart of a country of millions is a different beast itself. And yet time and again, God has intervened with decisions and leaders of nations.

44

John Adams

John Adams, second president of the United States, had the un-enviable and nearly impossible task of filling the shoes of a titan. In general, it did not go well, but if the four years Adams spent as president proved anything, it was that the nascent country had equipped itself to weather a storm and that democracy could manage a less-than-optimal choice without collapsing. Perhaps this doesn't give Adams enough credit for the crucial role he played in the country's foundation. No, he wasn't honored with a carving on Mount Rushmore or even a spot on our currency, but his early career opposing British policies, his voice in the rising revolution, and his leadership in early government were all essential to the foundation of the United States.

I pray Heaven to bestow the best of Blessings on this House and all that shall hereafter inhabit it. May none but honest and wise Men ever rule under this roof.

Why This Prayer?

Adams journaled and wrote prolifically, and the above was taken from a letter in 1800 sent home to his wife, Abigail. He'd just arrived at what was then called the President's House and was requesting God's blessing on all those who would take the charge to serve in the country's highest post. The sentiment was then carved into the state dining room mantel of the White House in 1945. If only two attributes could be guaranteed for every president, *honest* and *wise* would be two great choices.

45

JAMES MADISON

James Madison is known as a coauthor of the Federalist Papers, secretary of state under Thomas Jefferson, and the fourth president of the United States. He was president during the War of 1812, a complicated and problematic war we know mostly for giving us "The Star-Spangled Banner" as Francis Scott Key watched Fort McHenry get bombarded, and for the image of Madison's wife, Dolley, saving famous portraits from the White House when the British burned it. Madison was among the last of the founding fathers to serve as president and faced all the complications of a new country trying to establish itself as an international power.

Render him thanks for the many blessings he has bestowed on the people of the United States; that he has blessed them with a land capable of yielding all the necessaries and requisites of human life, with ample means for convenient exchanges with foreign countries; that he has blessed the labours employed in its cultivation and improvement; that he is now blessing the exertions to extend and establish the arts and manufactures, which will secure within ourselves supplies too important to remain dependent on the precarious policy, on the peaceable dispositions of other nations, and particularly that he has blessed the United States with a political constitution founded on the will and authority of the whole people, and guaranteeing to each individual the security, not only of his person and his property, but of those sacred rights of conscience, so essential to his present happiness, and so dear to his future hopes: that with those expressions of devout thankfulness be joined supplications to the same Almighty Power, that he would look down with compassion on our infirmities, that he would pardon our manifold transgressions, and awaken and strengthen in all the wholesome purposes of repentance and amendment; that in this season of trial and calamity, he would preside in a particular manner, over our public councils, and inspire all citizens with a love of their country, and with those fraternal affections and that mutual confidence, which have so happy a tendency to make us safe at home and respected abroad; and that, as he was graciously pleased, heretofore, to smile on our struggles against the attempts of the government of the empire, of which these states then made a part, to wrest from them the rights and privileges to which they were entitled in common with every other part, and to raise them to the station of an independent and sovereign people; so he would now be pleased, in like manner, to bestow his blessing on our arms in resisting the hostile and persevering efforts of the same power, to degrade us on the ocean, the common inheritance of all, from rights and immunities, belonging and essential to the American people, as a co-equal member of the great community of independent nations; and that, inspiring our enemies with moderation, with justice and with that spirit of reasonable accommodation, which our country has continued to manifest, we may be enabled to beat our swords into plough shares, and to enjoy in peace, every man, the fruits of his honest industry, and the rewards of his lawful enterprize.

WHY THIS PRAYER?

In this presidential proclamation, Madison declared a day of "Public Humiliation and Prayer," which is language one doesn't see very often these days. Writing his proclamation of topics that believers should pray over, he laid out the strengths of the country and the dangers it currently faced. The call, though, is not just for prayer but for a public display of humility and contrition. Perhaps it was more palatable at the time, as the war against Britain was a tedious slog with none of the glory of the Revolution. Few are the days our country is tasked with being humble now, and yet all need to be humble before God.

46

Franklin Delano Roosevelt

Franklin Delano Roosevelt served as president of the United States longer than any other person, from 1933 to 1945, overseeing a tumultuous time in the country's history and navigating the states through both the Great Depression and nearly the entirety of World War II. His administrations are responsible for the creation of Social Security and the Security and Exchange Commission among other government entities. Despite having a body frail from surviving polio, he stood strong in the face of fascism and Nazi Germany and helped the US and its allies defeat one of the darkest evils the world has ever seen.

Almighty God: Our sons, pride of our Nation, this day have set upon a mighty endeavor, a struggle to preserve our Republic, our religion, and our civilization, and to set free a suffering humanity.

Lead them straight and true; give strength to their arms, stoutness to their hearts, steadfastness in their faith.

They will need Thy blessings. Their road will be long and hard. For the enemy is strong. He may hurl back our forces. Success may not come with rushing speed, but we shall return again and again; and we know that by Thy grace, and by the righteousness of our cause, our sons will triumph.

They will be sore tried, by night and by day, without rest—until the victory is won. The darkness will be rent by noise and flame. Men's souls will be shaken with the violences of war.

For these men are lately drawn from the ways of peace. They fight not for the lust of conquest. They fight to end conquest. They fight to liberate. They fight to let justice arise, and tolerance and good will among all Thy people. They yearn but for the end of battle, for their return to the haven of home.

Some will never return. Embrace these, Father, and receive them, Thy heroic servants, into Thy kingdom.

And for us at home—fathers, mothers, children, wives, sisters, and brothers of brave men overseas—whose thoughts and prayers are ever with them—help us, Almighty God, to rededicate ourselves in renewed faith in Thee in this hour of great sacrifice.

Many people have urged that I call the Nation into a single day of special prayer. But because the road is long and the desire is great, I ask that our people devote themselves in a continuance of prayer. As we rise to each new day, and again when each day is spent, let words of prayer be on our lips, invoking Thy help to our efforts.

Give us strength, too—strength in our daily tasks, to redouble the contributions we make in the physical and the material support of our armed forces.

And let our hearts be stout, to wait out the long travail, to bear sorrows that may come, to impart our courage unto our sons where-soever they may be.

And, O Lord, give us Faith. Give us Faith in Thee; Faith in our sons; Faith in each other; Faith in our united crusade. Let not the keenness of our spirit ever be dulled. Let not the impacts of temporary events, of temporal matters of but fleeting moment let not these deter us in our unconquerable purpose.

With Thy blessing, we shall prevail over the unholy forces of our enemy. Help us to conquer the apostles of greed and racial arrogancies. Lead us to the saving of our country, and with our sister Nations *into a world unity that will spell a sure peace a peace invulnerable to the schemings of unworthy men. And a peace that will let all of men live in freedom, reaping the just rewards of their honest toil.*

Thy will be done, Almighty God.

Amen.

Why This Prayer?

Tuesday, June 6, 1944, is remembered as D-Day. Despite heavy German armaments up and down the Normandy coast, the Allied forces, including American, British, and Canadian forces, targeted five beaches on which to land and begin to push the Germans back on the European front. The scale of the invasion was enormous; more than twenty-four thousand soldiers landed, and it is still the largest invasion by sea ever. Roosevelt knew the importance of the moment in the war and knew that casualties could be particularly high. Delivered by radio, as were all of his important communications, this address from Roosevelt joined with all the families, all the citizens of the country, to pray. He prayed that our path as a country was true and that God would, as He has for centuries, honor the cause of a righteous war.

47

Jacob Duché

Born in Philadelphia in 1737, Jacob Duché is known primarily as saying the first prayer at the first gathering of the Continental Congress in 1774 and later serving as its first chaplain. He came to the position as rector of Christ Church in Philadelphia and has a complicated history in the early years of the United States. After the Declaration of Independence he joined a group that called for the removal of King George's name from the Book of Common Prayer and was later arrested by the British. By 1777, though, his political views had shifted, and in pushing for surrender to the British, he found himself charged with treason against Pennsylvania and fled to England, where he would remain nearly the rest of his life.

O Lord our Heavenly Father, high and mighty King of kings, and Lord of lords, who dost from thy throne behold all the dwellers on earth and reignest with power supreme and uncontrolled over all the Kingdoms, Empires and Governments; look down in mercy, we beseech Thee, on these our American States, who have fled to Thee from the rod of the oppressor and thrown themselves on Thy gracious protection, desiring to be henceforth dependent only on Thee. To Thee have they appealed for the righteousness of their cause; to Thee

*do they now look up for that countenance and support, which Thou
alone canst give. Take them, therefore, Heavenly Father, under Thy
nurturing care; give them wisdom in Council and valor in the field;
defeat the malicious designs of our cruel adversaries; convince them of
the unrighteousness of their Cause and if they persist in their sangui-
nary purposes, of own unerring justice, sounding in their hearts, con-
strain them to drop the weapons of war from their unnerved hands in
the day of battle!*

*Be Thou present, O God of wisdom, and direct the councils of this
honorable assembly; enable them to settle things on the best and surest
foundation. That the scene of blood may be speedily closed; that order,
harmony and peace may be effectually restored, and truth and justice,
religion and piety, prevail and flourish amongst the people. Preserve
the health of their bodies and vigor of their minds; shower down on
them and the millions they here represent, such temporal blessings
as Thou seest expedient for them in this world and crown them with
everlasting glory in the world to come. All this we ask in the name and
through the merits of Jesus Christ, Thy Son and our Savior.*

WHY THIS PRAYER?

The first prayer spoken over the group that founded the nation
was offered by a man who ultimately would be a traitor to the
cause about which he spoke. In the moment, however, the prayer
united and moved those in the room. The Continental Congress
had initially balked at even having a prayer, since so many faith
traditions were represented in the room. Eventually, however,
they agreed on its importance; after reading Psalm 35, Duché
surprised Congress by praying the words above from his heart.
They must have been exactly what was needed to be said, as John
Adams wrote his wife that the words "had an excellent effect on
everybody here."

48

WILLIAM PENN

Philadelphia and the state of Pennsylvania exist today—and have their names—because the king of England owed a debt to William Penn's father. In payment, he gave the Penn family the rights to the colonial land that would become Penn's namesake. William Penn sailed to the colonies numerous times in the late 1600s, eventually establishing the "City of Brotherly Love" along the Delaware River. Penn was a Quaker by faith, and the state was founded with many of the freedoms that would become the foundation of the Constitution over a century later, including democratic elections, freedom of religion, and trial by jury.

And Thou Philadelphia the virgin settlement of this province named before thou wert born, what care, what service, what travail have there been to bring thee forth and preserve thee from such as would abuse and defile thee. O that thou mayest be kept from the evil that would overwhelm thee, that faithful to the God of thy mercies in the life of righteousness, thou mayest be preserved to the end. My soul prays to God for thee that thou mayest stand in the day of trial, that thy children may be blest of the Lord and thy people saved by His power.

—————————— WHY THIS PRAYER? ——————————

The opportunity to pray over the founding of a city or state in our nation is hundreds of years in the past, and much has changed over the centuries. It's easy to simplify and make all of that history into legend, too, as though there was almost a special magic to the creation of the country. What's less important is focusing on these prayers as some kind of proof of America's specialness, and rather seeing them as a lesson for what it means to still pray for whatever place we call our home. Trials continue to come to cities and to our country. We seem, in some ways, far away from being a place of peace.

49

ABSALOM JONES

Born enslaved, Jones bought his freedom in 1784. A member of
St. George's Methodist Episcopal Church in Philadelphia, he and
Richard Allen's evangelism to the black community helped the
church grow quickly in membership. White congregants, however, pushed back on the growth, and when they tried to segre-
gate the new members, Jones and Allen and most of the black
congregants left. Together they formed The African Church and
the Free African Society, ministering in Philadelphia, particularly
during an outbreak of yellow fever. Allen would eventually split
to form the African Methodist Episcopal church, while Jones
remained as pastor of his church, renamed the African Episcopal Church of St. Thomas. The two stayed strong friends and
allies, however, and worked together for the complete abolition
of slavery in Pennsylvania and the country.

Oh thou God of all the nations upon the earth! We thank thee, that
thou art no respecter of persons, and that thou hast made of one
blood all nations of men. We thank thee, that thou hast appeared,
in the fulness of time, in behalf of the nation from which most of the
worshipping people, now before thee, are descended. We thank thee,
that the sun of righteousness has at last shed his morning beams

upon them. Rend thy heavens, O Lord, and come down upon the earth; and grant that the mountains, which now obstruct the perfect day of thy goodness and mercy towards them, may flow down at thy presence. Send thy gospel, we beseech thee, among them. May the nations, which now sit in darkness, behold and rejoice in its light. May Ethiopia soon stretch out her hands unto thee, and lay hold of the gracious promise of thy everlasting covenant. Destroy, we beseech thee, all the false religions which now prevail among them; and grant, that they may soon cast their idols, to the moles and the bats of the wilderness. O, hasten that glorious time, when the knowledge of the gospel of Jesus Christ, shall cover the earth, as the waters cover the sea; when the wolf shall dwell with the lamb, and the leopard shall lie down with the kid, and the calf and the young lion and the fatling together, and a little child shall lead them; and, when, instead of the thorn, shall come up the fir tree, and, instead of the brier, shall come up the myrtle tree: and it shall be to the Lord for a name and for an everlasting sign that shall not be cut off. We pray, O God, for all our friends and benefactors, in Great Britain, as well as in the United States: reward them, we beseech thee, with blessings upon earth, and prepare them to enjoy the fruits of their kindness to us, in thy everlasting kingdom in heaven: and dispose us, who are assembled in thy presence, to be always thankful for thy mercies, and to act as becomes a people who owe so much to thy goodness. We implore thy blessing, O God, upon the President, and all who are in authority in the United States. Direct them by thy wisdom, in all their deliberations, and O save thy people from the calamities of war. Give peace in our day, we beseech thee, O thou God of peace! and grant, that this highly favoured country may continue to afford a safe and peaceful retreat from the calamities of war and slavery, for ages yet to come. We implore all these blessings and mercies, only in the name of thy beloved Son, Jesus Christ, our Lord. And now, O Lord, we desire, with angels and arch-angels, and all the company of heaven, ever more to praise thee, saying, Holy, holy, holy, Lord God Almighty: the whole earth is full of thy glory. Amen.

─────────WHY THIS PRAYER?─────────

On January 1, 1808, Absalom Jones preached a sermon at St. Thomas's that concluded with this prayer. Congress had voted that the African slave trade be abolished, effective on that date, ending at least one horrifying chapter of slavery's corrupt place in US culture. At that time, though, any win on behalf of abolition was seen as a significant milestone. Jones lifts up not only his country but the continent of Africa as well for God's blessings. Jones's own life was blessed and changed by God's grace, and his compelling vision for the Good News to go out into the world is one that we share today. That *all* may hear of God's love and *all* may know of Jesus' sacrifice.

PRAYERS
in the FACE *of* PAIN
and GRIEF

But you, God, see the trouble of the afflicted;
you consider their grief and take it in hand.

Psalm 10:14

50

WILLIAM TYNDALE

A martyr to the reign of Henry VIII, Tyndale—one of the many "Jesus freaks" throughout history who paid such a price—spoke out against the corruption of religion by the political rulers and paid for holding true to his beliefs. Prior to his death, Tyndale was best known as a Protestant reformer and for his role in early translations of the Bible into English.

Lord, open the King of England's eyes!

WHY THIS PRAYER?

Tradition holds that these were among Tyndale's last words as he faced execution. Henry VIII manipulated religion to whatever suited his needs, whether it was breaking from the Catholic Church to form the Church of England or forcing the church to abide by his whims relating to his marriage and divorce. Truth was what Henry declared rather than anything tied to Scripture or Jesus' teachings, and those like Thomas More and Tyndale who opposed him paid for doing so. The Church does not need to stand apart from political power, but too often it has been abused by those who have no intention of living by the precepts of Christian faith. The Bible has been used by evil men to defend slavery, and the Holocaust, and the oppression of millions. Tyndale's last cry for the king to see God's truth didn't prevent his death, but it's never a prayer we can stop praying.

51

LUDWIG VAN BEETHOVEN

You know Ludwig van Beethoven's compositions whether you recognize them by name or not. His Fifth Symphony as well as his Ninth Symphony, known colloquially as "Ode to Joy," are both among the most instantly recognizable pieces in human history. When Henry van Dyke penned the lyrics to "The Hymn of Joy" in 1907, poetically setting the words "joyful, joyful, we adore Thee" to Beethoven's melody, it became a rousing hymn that used music and verse to praise God. The Ninth Symphony was written, as most know, when Beethoven was deaf. His hearing had begun failing in the early 1800s and continued to deteriorate, seriously influencing his career. The music lived in him, though, and found expression in a world-changing way.

O God give me strength to be victorious over myself, for nothing may chain me to this life. O guide my spirit, O raise me from these dark depths, that my soul, transported through Thy wisdom, may fearlessly struggle upward in fiery flight. For Thou alone understandest and canst inspire me.

——————— WHY THIS PRAYER? ———————

There are prayers we offer in moments of crisis, shouts and bursts of need, and then there are the hard prayers that follow us, day after week after month after year after decade sometimes. They are prayers during difficult things—broken relationships, wounded bodies, lost loves, hurting minds—that find no quick reply or solution. Beethoven's life is an example of this, and we can hear the pain in his words. There are unlimited easy and cheap platitudes that we can relate to those who are hurting, and it seems they can sometimes do more harm than good. "Let go and let God" is not something from which Beethoven would have taken any comfort. Still he sought God, still he fought for comfort, for peace amid his struggles. He lifted his words to God and set an example for our darkest days.

52

CLARA ANN THOMPSON

Clara Ann Thompson lived nearly all her life in Rossmoyne, Ohio, outside of Cincinnati. Born shortly after the end of the Civil War, Thompson's parents were former enslaved people who'd moved from Virginia to Ohio. Thompson became a well-regarded poet and advocate for civil rights. She had her own printing press and self-published her most well-known volume, *Songs From the Wayside*, which included numerous religious poems.

> *Out of the deep, I cry to Thee, oh Lord!*
> *Out of the deep of darkness, and distress;*
> *I cannot, will not doubt Thy blessed word,*
> *Oh, God of righteousness!*
>
> *I cry, and oh, my God, I know Thou'lt heed,*
> *For Thou hast promised Thou wouldst heed my cry;*
> *I have no words to tell my deepest need,*
> *Thou knowest oh, Most High!*
>
> *Thou knowest all the pain,—the agony,*
> *The grief I strive so vainly to express;*

Oh let Thy shelt'ring wings spread over me,
Great God of tenderness!

I cannot, cannot cease to cry to Thee,
For oh, my God, this heart is not my own,
And as the streams press ever to the sea,
My heart turns to Thy throne.

And when too weak to lift my voice, I lie
In utter silence at Thy blessed feet,
Thou'lt know, that silence is my deepest cry,
Thy throne, my last retreat.

And shouldst Thou hide Thy face for aye, from me,
My heart, though shattered, evermore would grope
Out through the darkness, still in search of Thee,
Oh God, my only hope!

WHY THIS PRAYER?

This is the cry of a heart's lament. It reflects the imagery in Psalm 27, when David, searching for God in the midst of deep trials, pleads for the Lord to not hide His face. The point of a poem and prayer like this isn't to know what event sparked the words but to feel the echo in our own lives. Thompson writes of a heart that, especially when broken, turns to where it belongs—to God. When we like prodigal children wander off during good times and lose our way, pains will invariably get us facing true north again.

53

RICHARD ALLEN

Richard Allen founded the oldest official African American organization in the United States, the African Methodist Episcopal (AME) Church. Born into slavery, Allen became a Christian as a teen, through the ministry of itinerant Methodist preachers, and soon began his own preaching. Allen was given the opportunity to buy his freedom, and once free, he was invited to become a pastor to a Philadelphia congregation that quickly became torn by segregation. He formed his own church, Bethel African Methodist Episcopal Church, and in 1816 helped officially form the AME denomination. His family home was a station on the Underground Railroad, and he and his wife were devoted to ministry to the community until his death in 1831.

> O, my God! In all my dangers, temporal and spiritual, I will hope in Thee who art Almighty power, and therefore able to relieve me; who are infinite goodness, and therefore ready and willing to assist me. . . . What, though I moan and am afflicted here, and sigh under the miseries of this world for a time, I am sure that my tears shall one day be turned into joy, and that joy none shall take from me.

WHY THIS PRAYER?

As an enslaved person, Allen knew hard times, difficult days of which we can hardly conceive. When looking at struggles and difficulties, we need balance. We can't turn molehills into mountains, but nor do we pretend that our lives must be perfect simply because others have it harder. Our fears, our anxieties, our pains, our broken dreams—they are the wounds that we carry. The promise—that not only does God offer relief now but complete joy in His eternal presence—impacts us all.

54

BENJAMIN TUCKER TANNER

Beginning in 1868, Benjamin Tucker Tanner was editor of the *Christian Recorder* for the AME church, one of the oldest periodicals published by African Americans in the country. He also helped establish religious instruction for freed slaves in Washington, DC, supported missionary work in Haiti, and pastored churches in Baltimore and Georgetown.

To Thee, oh Lord, we make our plea
That human sorrows thou wouldst see
And human grief; and human tears
That flow throughout the life-long years

Awake o Lord and speak the word,
Awake, assert thyself as Lord
And let the pain of head and heart
At thy dear comings Lord depart

Awake, and let thy people know
That from them thou wilt never go;
And let the world be put to shame—
If, Lord, it rev'rence not thy name.

WHY THIS PRAYER?

Again and again, we hear testimony about how it is in times of pain and suffering that God often feels closest, or manifests most fully in people's lives. Less spoken of are the times we feel most alone and hopeless in our trials. They are not triumphant moments of faith, and so a spotlight is not shone on them, but sometimes it is too easy to stare into the darkness without turning to the light. We need to know these human moments of despair are just that—human and moments. They are borne of lies we believe that God might not listen, might not draw near. But they are just that . . . lies. God is awake, is always listening. When we give Him our voice, put words to our pain, and rest in Him, those lies are put to shame and we find our comfort in the One who never leaves us.

55

JOSEPHINE D. HEARD

Josephine Heard's collection of poetry, *Morning Glories*, offers a glimpse into her life and faith. She wrote of her deep love of teaching, a passion she came to as a young woman and pursued throughout her life. After her marriage to William Henry Heard, an AME pastor, the two moved from city to city in his ministry, with Josephine teaching wherever they landed.

> *My God, sometimes I cannot pray,*
> *Nor can I tell why thus I weep;*
> *The words my heart has framed I cannot say,*
> *Behold me prostrate at Thy feet.*
>
> *Thou understandest all my woe;*
> *Thou knows't the craving of my soul—*
> *Thine eye beholdeth whereso'er I go;*
> *Thou can'st this wounded heart make whole.*
>
> *And oh! while prostrate here I lie,*
> *And groan the words I fain would speak:*
> *Unworthy though I be, pass not me by,*
> *But let Thy love in showers break.*

And deluge all my thirsty soul,
And lay my proud ambition low;
So while time's billows o'er me roll,
I shall be washed as white as snow.

Thou wilt not quench the smoking flax,
Nor wilt thou break the bruised reed;
Like potter's clay, or molten wax,
Mould me to suit Thy will indeed.

WHY THIS PRAYER?

This poem from Heard eloquently puts to words those heartsick times when we are overwhelmed and can only feel rather than speak. It redefines prayer as not just a conversation but as the longing needs of our heart, which God knows even in our silence. Words uttered or recited that we do not believe may sound like prayer to those listening, but God hears and understands even when we can't find the right thing to say. He is waiting only for our spirits to turn to Him.

56

BOOK *of* COMMON PRAYER— FUNERAL PRAYER

These are words we've likely heard before—"ashes to ashes and dust to dust." Perhaps you've been at a funeral where they were spoken. Perhaps you've read them or seen them in a movie portrayal of a funeral. They've entered our common parlance, an adaptation of the words of Scripture from Genesis 3:19—"By the sweat of your brow you will eat your food until you return to the ground, since from it you were taken; for dust you are and to dust you will return." They are part of the consequences laid out by God after Adam and Eve's disobedience in the Garden of Eden. Toil, pain, and death. He breathed life into dead earth and we emerged, but now we would return. All of us. Even Jesus was laid in a tomb, returned to the ground. Only Jesus, though, broke the curse.

In sure and certain hope of the resurrection to eternal life through our Lord Jesus Christ, we commend to Almighty God our [brother/sister], and we commit his body to the ground; earth to earth, ashes to ashes, dust to dust. The Lord bless him and keep him, the Lord make his face to shine upon him and be gracious to him, the Lord lift up his countenance upon him and give him peace. Amen.

———— Why This Prayer? ————

The "sure and certain hope of the resurrection" should be the famous phrase from this prayer, rather than the somber intonation of "ashes to ashes, dust to dust." For that hope—and the confidence therein—is the very substance of grace. The somber words are for the grieving, those left to stand by the grave of the deceased, and they do, quite often, match our mood and spirit. For the dead, though, neither earth nor ash nor dust mean anything. The Lord lifts His countenance upon us at our death, and Jesus' saving work is made complete. We are blessed and kept in His presence, now and forevermore. Amen.

PRAYERS
for FAITH *to* BE
STRENGTHENED

So do not fear, for I am with you; do not be dismayed, for
I am your God. I will strengthen you and help you; I will
uphold you with my righteous right hand.

Isaiah 41:10

57

APOSTLES' CREED

The legend behind the name of this ancient creed is that each of Jesus' original twelve disciples contributed a tenet to its construction, hence its twelve articles of faith. Ignoring the fact that this would include something from Judas, which seems less than ideal, the truth behind its construction is lost to history. Instead, what remains is a concise recitation of the core and critical beliefs of Christianity—what C. S. Lewis would one day call "mere."

> *I believe in God, the Father almighty, maker of heaven and earth;*
> *And in Jesus Christ, his only Son, Our Lord; who was conceived by the Holy Ghost, born of the Virgin Mary, suffered under Pontius Pilate, was crucified, dead, and buried. He descended into hell. The third day he rose again from the dead. He ascended into heaven, and sitteth on the right hand of God the Father almighty. From thence he shall come to judge the quick and the dead.*
> *I believe in the Holy Ghost, the holy catholic Church, the communion of saints, the forgiveness of sins, the resurrection of the body, and the life everlasting. Amen.*

─────── Why This Prayer? ───────

This is not a prayer, obviously, in the traditional sense. But whether it's something you've only ever read on the page, a weekly piece of liturgy recited along with other congregants, or something in between, it's a critical confession of belief that God hears with joy. "I believe . . . I believe . . ." we offer, and as the word is repeated, we affirm not only our faith but that faith has never flickered out. We are part of the small *c* "holy catholic Church," which has stretched from the first days of Acts to the very moment you're reading these words. Amen.

58

ANDREW MURRAY

The legacy of Andrew Murray remains mostly in the vast trove of writings he left, with more than two hundred published. Born in 1828, Murray pastored for the Dutch Reformed Church at various parishes throughout South Africa and helped lead a revival there in the 1860s. He is perhaps best known for *Humility: The Journey Toward Holiness* as well as *Absolute Surrender* and *Abide in Christ*.

Blessed Saviour! with my whole heart I do bless Thee for the appointment of the inner chamber, as the school where Thou meetest each of Thy pupils alone, and revealest to him the Father. O my Lord! strengthen my faith so in the Father's tender love and kindness, that as often as I feel sinful or troubled, the first instinctive thought may be to go where I know the Father waits me, and where prayer never can go unblessed. Let the thought that He knows my need before I ask, bring me, in great restfulness of faith, to trust that He will give what His child requires. O let the place of secret prayer become to me the most beloved spot of earth.

And, Lord! hear me as I pray that Thou wouldest everywhere bless the closets of Thy believing people. Let Thy wonderful revelation of a Father's tenderness free all young Christians from every thought of secret prayer as a duty or a burden, and lead them to regard it as the highest privilege of their life, a joy and a blessing. Bring back all who are discouraged, because they cannot find ought to bring Thee in prayer. O give them to understand that they have only to come with their emptiness to Him who has all to give, and delights to do it. Not, what they have to bring the Father, but what the Father waits to give them, be their one thought.

WHY THIS PRAYER?

That we have the opportunity to pray directly to God is perhaps a wonder we too often take for granted. While men and women certainly cried out to God prior to Jesus, the mechanics of approaching God involved rituals of sacrifice and complex rules high priests had been carrying out since the days of Moses. Jesus, in His Sermon on the Mount, invokes the inner sanctum—which Murray references above—by encouraging believers that they should find a secret place to worship God alone. Then He died, and the temple veil was torn in two, highlighting even more dramatically that the old ways of approaching the Father were over. Jesus is our high priest now, and we have every confidence that God meets us in our closets, our inner sanctums, when we approach Him. Even when we have no idea what to say and can only offer ourselves.

59

JOHN CALVIN

Born in France in 1509, John Calvin, another of the early reform-
ers of the Church, trained as a lawyer before devoting his life to
the life of the spirit as theologian and minister among the growing Protestant churches. Calvin's theological musings became
known as Calvinism. He was a prolific writer, and his complete
work of biblical commentaries is a masterwork of religious texts.

*O LORD, who art the fountain of all wisdom and learning, since thou
of thy special goodness hast granted that my youth is instructed in
good arts which may assist me to honest and holy living, grant also, by
enlightening my mind, which otherwise labors under blindness, that
I may be fit to acquire knowledge; strengthen my memory faithfully
to retain what I may have learned: and govern my heart, that I may
be willing and even eager to profit, lest the opportunity which thou
now givest me be lost through my sluggishness. Be pleased therefore to
infuse thy Spirit into me, the Spirit of understanding, of truth, judgment, and prudence, lest my study be without success, and the labour
of my teacher be in vain.*

*In whatever kind of study I engage, enable me to remember to keep
its proper end in view, namely, to know thee in Christ Jesus thy Son;
and may every thing that I learn assist me to observe the right rule of*

godliness. And seeing thou promisest that thou wilt bestow wisdom on babes, and such as are humble, and the knowledge of thyself on the upright in heart, while thou declarest that thou wilt cast down the wicked and the proud, so that they will fade away in their ways, I entreat that thou wouldst be pleased to turn me to true humility, that thus I may show myself teachable and obedient first of all to thyself, and then to those also who by thy authority are placed over me. Be pleased at the same time to root out all vicious desires from my heart, and inspire it with an earnest desire of seeking thee. Finally, let the only end at which I aim be so to qualify myself in early life, that when I grow up I may serve thee in whatever station thou mayest assign me. Amen.

Why This Prayer?

While the fear of the Lord is the beginning of wisdom, it is not the end nor the completion of wisdom. There is much in the world to know, and God has given us curiosity and intelligence and sharp minds to puzzle out His creation. Calvin's prayer puts God where the Bible puts Him—at the beginning of wisdom. He does not fit *alongside* our understanding of math or science or all of humanity but is the worldview *through* which we understand math's intricate perfection or the amazing complexity of the human body or anything. The prayer calls for us to be humble and teachable—we have infinity out ahead of us and should never forget there is always more to learn, at any age.

60

GEORGE WHITEFIELD

Born in England in 1714, George Whitefield eventually made his way to the colonies in the 1740s, preaching to millions as one of the chief voices of the Great Awakening. This massive revival took hold in the American colonies for over a decade as the spirit worked through the land. Serving as a counterpoint to the Enlightenment movement earlier in the century, this was a movement back to the spirit and God's Word and Whitefield was a key figure, traveling up and down the colonies, and preaching as many as three-hundred and fifty times in a year. Whitefield was not part of a particular denomination, but soon became linked with the Methodist movement along with the Wesleys and Charles Finney.

Yea . . . that we shall see the great Head of the Church once more bring into being His special instruments of revival, that He will again raise up unto Himself certain young men whom He may use in this glorious employ. And what manner of men will they be? Men mighty in the Scriptures, their lives dominated by a sense of the greatness, the majesty and holiness of God, and their minds and hearts aglow with the great truths of the doctrines of grace. They will be men who have learned what it is to die to self, to human aims and personal ambitions; men who are willing to be "fools for Christ's sake," who will bear reproach and falsehood, who will labor and suffer, and whose supreme desire will be, not to gain earth's accolades, but to win the Master's approbation when they appear before His awesome judgment seat. They will be men who will preach with broken hearts and tear-filled eyes, and upon whose ministries God will grant an extraordinary effusion of the Holy Spirit, and who will witness "signs and wonders following" in the transformation of multitudes of human lives.

WHY THIS PRAYER?

Living as a Christian is something outside of time or place. Jesus is not only relevant to first-century Greeks or nineteenth-century Brits. He is for every time and every locale. And yet, the expression of Christianity is certainly tied to the time and place a person lives. Though we try to be "not in the world," we are human and are shaped, even in ways we don't understand, by the cultures in which we are raised. The Great Awakening and George Whitefield and the other voices in the movement played a large part in shaping religion in the United States—not just in the early 1700s but still through today. We see the roots of many different offshoots of the American church in the movement and hear, in Whitefield's words, a similarly modern call to raise up true believers. This call cannot be that different from that of the church in Acts as signs and wonders abounded. Hundreds of years apart, and both the same and different, prayers echo through history.

61

JOHN CHRYSOSTOM

An early church leader, John Chrysostom was archbishop of Constantinople . . . though not by choice. While living in Antioch he had gained a reputation as an eloquent preacher—*Chrysostom* actually is a nickname that means "golden-voiced"—and church authorities became convinced that the greatest city should have the greatest people in it. Soldiers transported him to that important city, where his sermons condemning the trappings of wealth and power eventually got him exiled until his death in 407.

Remember, O Lord, this city wherein we dwell and every other city and country, and all the faithful who dwell in them. Remember, O Lord, all who travel by land or water, all that labour under sickness or slavery; remember them for health and safety. Remember, O Lord, those in Thy Holy Church who bring forth good fruit, are rich in good works and forget not the poor. Grant unto us all Thy mercy and loving-kindness, and grant that we may with one mouth and one heart praise and glorify Thy great and glorious name, Father, Son, and Holy Ghost, now, henceforth, and forever. Amen.

────── WHY THIS PRAYER? ──────

The vision of the Church that John Chrysostom presents here—praising God with one mouth and heart—is a powerful representation of what can unify us. In especially difficult times, it's easy to focus on the things that divide, but when we turn our lives to God, we are more the same than different. The things that seemed so big look tiny compared to God, and such a vision returns our focus to Him, where it should have been all along.

62

St. Basil

Bishop of Caesarea—modern-day Turkey—in 370, St. Basil (or Basil the Great) was a powerful voice in the early Church. Numerous works from his pen have survived, including collected sermons and writings aimed at monastic life and his *Address to Young Men*. Basil is one of the three Cappadocian Fathers, saints crucial in championing and maintaining traditional Christian theology, including the doctrine of the Trinity.

O Lord our God, teach us, we beseech Thee, to ask Thee aright for the right blessings. Steer Thou the vessel of our life toward Thyself, Thou tranquil Haven of all storm-tossed souls. Show us the course wherein we should go. Renew a willing spirit within us. Let Thy Spirit curb our wayward senses, and guide and enable us unto that which is our true good, to keep Thy laws, and in all our works evermore to rejoice in Thy glorious and gladdening Presence. For Thine is the glory and praise from all Thy saints forever and ever—Amen.

Why This Prayer?

The path through life for a person seeking to be led by God can be a fraught journey. The pressure to make each decision "right" can sometimes feel overwhelming, particularly in a season when God doesn't feel near. St. Basil offers a prayer that reminds us it is less about the journey and more about abiding in Christ that is important. If we are with God, we are in the right spot no matter the path that got us there.

63

POLYCARP

Polycarp was among the second generation of believers in the early Church, men and women who heard the Good News from the original disciples and became important figures in sustaining the Church. Tradition holds that he knew and learned from the disciple John and eventually was installed as bishop of the church in Smyrna, in what is now Turkey. One letter survives that he wrote. Polycarp was eventually put to death by Rome at the age of 86.

> *But may the God and Father of our Lord Jesus Christ, and Jesus Christ Himself, who is the Son of God, and our everlasting High Priest, build you up in faith and truth, and in all meekness, gentleness, patience, long-suffering, forbearance, and purity; and may He bestow on you a lot and portion among His saints, and on us with you, and on all that are under heaven, who shall believe in our Lord Jesus Christ, and in His Father, who raised Him from the dead.*

—— WHY THIS PRAYER? ——

Taken from Polycarp's letter to the church of the Philippians, this is not just a call for the fruit of the Spirit to be made more evident in our lives—although that's certainly a piece of the prayer. It's a list we likely would not pray over ourselves too often. Meekness, gentleness, patience, forbearance . . . these are not traits or attributes that receive much respect in our modern, fast-paced world, though they are attributes we're called to live out. Beyond the list, though, this is another reminder that our prayers are offered in Jesus' name as both Son of God and Eternal High Priest. Hebrews offers that Jesus is a priest in the order of Melchizedek, both because He ends the line of priests from Aaron forever and also because He's both king and priest at the same time. Jesus is the ultimate fulfilment of Old Testament prophecy and the One who, as priest and sacrifice both, forever ends the transactional nature of our relationship with God, leaving us only with grace and the good news of His lasting salvation.

64

HANNAH WHITALL SMITH

Born and raised as a Quaker, Hannah Whitall Smith underwent a spiritual transformation in her twenties and became a popular and well-regarded speaker and evangelist in America and Britain in the late 1800s along with her husband, Robert. She wrote the Holiness movement work *The Christian's Secret of a Happy Life*, which sold millions. Hannah also helped found the Woman's Christian Temperance Union and fought for women's suffrage.

I give you my heart, Lord, to love only what you love; to hate what you hate; to endure all things, to suffer long and be kind, to be not easily provoked; to think no evil, not to seek my own. Help me, oh my God!

I give you my intellect to be wholly devoted to your service, and perfectly under your control to think only whose thoughts that will please you, to devise only such plans as you suggest, to yield the management of all its affairs to you! I give it to you that you may fulfill the purposes of your grace by casting down in me imaginations, and every high thing that exalts itself against the knowledge of God, and bringing into captivity every thought to the obedience of Christ. Help me, oh my God.

I give you my body to be used by you. My eyes to see only what you would have them see, my ears to hear only what you would have them hear; my feet to go only where you lead, my hands to do only what can be done in fellowship with you, my tongue to speak only words that please you. I give you any appetite to be under thy control and regulation. I give my time to you, Lord, to be all employed for you.

I leave my reputation in your hands. I give you my children, my husband, and everyone whom I love to be disposed of according to your will. I leave to you the ordering of my whole life, and with your help will follow you wherever you lead. I will give you the control of my feelings and of my prejudices.

I submit, in short, my whole being and life all that I am and have and will be to your complete control and only ask that your will may be perfectly done in me, through me and by me! Take me and keep me oh my God!

Why This Prayer?

Pulled from Smith's journal, this prayer can inspire us to name the things in our lives we want to consecrate to God. It might be a similar list—our body and mind, our family and loved ones. It might be more focused based on what we're facing—our house and home when we're feeling called to be hospitable. Our money when we're feeling pinched about our stinginess. Anything—everything—can and should be consecrated to God. He wants all of us, and what we try to keep from Him risks becoming a worthless idol that we clutch as though it has any power to save us.

65

St. Ignatius Loyola

Born Iñigo López de Oñaz y Loyola in the Basque region of Spain, St. Ignatius devoted his life to Christ while recovering from a battle wound and left with only religious books to read. Changed in heart, he began living an ascetic life and began a period of studying, which led him to France, where he met, among others, Peter Faber and Francis Xavier. Together, they founded the order of the Jesuits. Approved by Rome in 1540, this lasting organization, the Society of Jesus, set up schools and charities and mission outposts around the world.

> *Teach us, good Lord to serve thee as thou deservest,*
> *to give and not to count the cost;*
> *to fight and not to heed the wounds;*
> *to toil and not to seek for rest;*
> *to labor and not to ask for any reward;*
> *except that of knowing that we do thy will. Amen.*

Why This Prayer?

Too often in life our focus is on the blessings God promises. Our brains are wired to respond to pleasure and reward. We seek them readily, and yet that's not entirely the life to which God calls us. As Ignatius points out, we are also called to give of ourselves. Those sacrifices will be of time, of energy, and in difficult cases, sometimes even of our lives. We give ourselves to God as His tools to be used to shape the kingdom. If you use any tool, you know it's rare for it to be returned as new and pristine as it came out of the box. We will be changed as much in the process as the change we bring, but living in God's will makes those wounds, nicks on our heart, and scabs on our spirit become badges of courage for trusting God.

PRAYERS *of* THANKSGIVING *and* GRATITUDE

Rejoice always, pray continually, give thanks in all circumstances; for this is God's will for you in Christ Jesus.

1 Thessalonians 5:16–18

66

MARTIN LUTHER

Born in Germany in 1483, Martin Luther's towering role in the history of the Christian Church is hard to overstate. Luther's split with his upbringing and ordination as a Catholic priest came from a return of focus on the primacy of God rather than the established Church. Rejecting the call for manipulative use of indulgences and the unattainable finish line of a salvation based on works, Luther focused on Jesus and His offer of saving grace. His "protest," nailed to the Wittenberg church door, split the church irrevocably and gave rise to countless denominations to come, including one bearing Luther's own name.

> *My Heavenly Father, I thank You, through Jesus Christ, Your beloved Son, that You have protected me, by Your grace. Forgive, I pray, all my sins and the evil I have done. Protect me, by Your grace, tonight. I put myself in your care, body and soul and all that I have. Let Your holy angels be with me, so that the evil enemy will not gain power over me. Amen.*

—————— WHY THIS PRAYER? ——————

Trained and educated as a priest, Luther's critique of the Church was not about liturgy, and he continued to see value in many of the traditions, including morning and evening prayer. The above is a concise and all-encompassing evening prayer that can be said on your knees, bedside. When we pause to reflect on our day, giving thanks and offering praise, the depths of night loom less like a descent into darkness and more as an opportunity for rest and recovery, trusting God with our all, body and soul.

67

Anne Bradstreet

A Puritan born in 1612, Anne Bradstreet sailed to America in 1630 as part of the founding of the Massachusetts Bay Colony. Bradstreet was already married at the time and ended up the mother of eight children. She is best known as being one of the first colonists to be published, and her poetry is some of the earliest colonial writings that have survived. Faith and family stood at the heart of the majority of her poems.

> *O thou that hear'st the prayers of Thine*
> *And 'mongst them hast regarded mine,*
> *Hast heard my cries and seen my tears,*
> *Hast known my doubts and all my fears,*
> *Thou hast relieved my fainting heart*
> *Nor paid me after my desert;*
> *Thou hast to shore him safely brought*
> *For whom I Thee so oft besought.*
> *Thou wast the pilot to the ship,*
> *And raised him up when he was sick,*
> *And hope Thou'st given of good success*
> *In this his business and address,*
> *And that Thou wilt return him back*

Whose presence I so much do lack.
For all these mercies I Thee praise
And so desire ev'n all my days.

—————— WHY THIS PRAYER? ——————

What is so often missing from the prayers of history are the very specific, timely prayers for God's hand to guide and protect one's loved ones in a specific moment. It's mostly because these prayers feel so important that we're more likely to say them than to write them. But in facing illness or danger or long journeys, our prayers have never changed. Bradstreet's prayer above found the page after hearing from her husband that he'd arrived safely back in England for a meeting with the king. One can only imagine the helplessness of watching a loved one board a boat for another transatlantic journey at that time. Her only hope—our only hope if we're honest—was in God's guiding hand. All our doubts and fears are His—the peace He can offer at our most difficult times is a good and perfect gift.

68

PRAYERS *of* GRACE *for* MEALS

The provenance of all of these prayers is lost to history, but each is an example of a simple grace that families have spoken over food for decades if not centuries. When a prayer is repeated, day after day and meal after meal, there is always the danger that its meaning will be lost and it will simply become words. But the message at the heart of each of these prayers, simple as they may be, is unimpeachable. As families link hands around the table, the words link them all in a tradition that carries beyond that moment and ties into the importance that breaking bread has always had in the Church.

> *God is great, God is good, let us thank Him for our food.*
> *By His hands we all are fed, give us Lord our daily bread.*
> *Amen.*

> *Come, Lord Jesus, be our Guest,*
> *and let these gifts to us be blessed.*
> *Amen.*

Bless us, O Lord, and these, thy gifts,
which we are about to receive from thy bounty,
through Christ, our Lord,
Amen.

Lord, we thank you for the food before us, the friends beside
    us,
the love between us, and your presence among us.
Amen.

WHY THESE PRAYERS?

Perhaps you said one of these prayers while at the dinner table growing up. Or had a meal with a friend, and their whole family bowed their heads to say words of thanks. But we don't call these short prayers *thanks*, we call them *grace* instead. The lineage of the word comes from the Latin *gratiarum actio*, which means *thanksgiving* and leads to words like *grazie* ("thanks") in Italian. *Grace* is a loaded word in English for the Church, though, hinting at so much more. Perhaps it's right that the word echoes all that comes from perhaps the most famous meal in the Bible, when Jesus broke bread and shared the cup with His disciples on the cusp of true grace entering the world at His death. In the meantime, these simple prayers continue to be part of families' spiritual heritages as easy poems to teach children to be thankful and ways for entire families to stop a moment and remember all we've been given.

69

St. Richard
of Chichester

Appointed Bishop of Chichester, England, in 1244, Richard de Wyche found himself opposed by the king. Henry III preferred a different candidate, and he not only confiscated the property and belongings of the parish but refused to return them for over two years, despite pressure from the Vatican. Richard relied on the charity of the members of his parish during that time, until the king finally relented in 1247. From the cathedral in Chichester, he became a tireless advocate for those in need, his own years of poverty creating a humble spirit and lifestyle that did not change even when his title was acknowledged.

> *Thanks be to thee, my Lord Jesus Christ,*
> *for all the benefits thou hast given me,*
> *for all the pains and insults thou hast borne for me.*
> *O most merciful redeemer, friend and brother,*
> *may I know thee more clearly,*
> *love thee more dearly,*
> *and follow thee more nearly, day by day.*
> *Amen.*

— Why This Prayer? —

You may recognize a portion of the prayer, perhaps can even sing the tune written by Stephen Schwartz for *Godspell* that accompanied a version of these words as lyrics. Fewer know that the actual prayer is more than seven hundred years old and attributed to a modest English bishop, who supposedly prayed these words through his life and then on his deathbed. While the famous words of the song now sound almost cliché, they are all the more powerful for knowing what trials Richard of Chichester faced early in his career. Refused his home and salary for years, he knew that the insults were not his alone to bear. Pains, sorrows, insults, worries—they all rest on the shoulders of Jesus, if we allow Him to take those burdens from us. And each day brings another opportunity—to forget this blessing and feel the overwhelming weight on our own, or to remember that blessing and thrive.

70

JOHN GREENLEAF WHITTIER

John Greenleaf Whittier gained enough notoriety for his poetry in his life that he was asked to pen words for the Washington centenary celebration in 1889, in recognition of the first president's inauguration. Born in Massachusetts in 1807, Whittier was raised Quaker, and his religious upbringing infuses many of his poems—some of which later became hymns when others put them to music. His poems often addressed the issue of abolition, as well, as Whittier became a strong advocate for the movement and was one of the original members of the American Anti-Slavery Society.

All things are thine; no gift have we,
Lord of all gifts, to offer thee;
and so with grateful hearts today
thine own before thy feet we lay.
Thy will was informed builders' thought;
thy hand unseen amidst us wrought;
through mortal motive, scheme, and plan,
thy wise eternal purpose ran.

No lack thy perfect fullness knew;
for human needs and longings grew
this house of prayer, this home of rest,
where grace is shared and truth addressed.
In weakness and in want, we call
on thee for whom the heavens are small;
thy glory is thy children's good,
thy joy fulfilled in servanthood.

All things are thine; no gift have we,
Lord of all gifts, to offer thee;
and so with grateful hearts today
thine own before thy feet we lay.
Come now and deign these walls to bless;
fill with thy love their emptiness;
and let their door a gateway be
to lead us from ourselves to thee.

WHY THIS PRAYER?

When we think of blessings from the Lord, very often we think of answered prayers to physical or earthly needs. We think of a request for a healed illness, or a prayer lifted on behalf of a family member struggling with unemployment, or the quiet ask, over and over, to finally conceive. There are infinite things for which we can ask—infinite ways God can reach out and touch our lives—and we have nothing to offer in return. Nothing that doesn't come from God originally, at least. Our love comes from Him. Our faith is taught to us by Him. Our hearts are closed until He opens the door that lets in the Spirit. If we aren't offering everything back to God, we don't truly understand how much we've been given.

71

PAUL LAURENCE DUNBAR

In 1893, poet Paul Dunbar published his first book of poems, *Oak and Ivy*, and came to Chicago to find work at the World's Fair. There he met Frederick Douglass, who arranged an opportunity for the young man to read his poetry. Soon after, Dunbar's verse began appearing nationally in newspapers and magazines, certainly making him one of the foremost African American poets of the time. He published a number of collections of poems, and essays, novels, and short stories as well, before his untimely death at thirty-three.

The sun hath shed its kindly light,
Our harvesting is gladly o'er,
Our fields have felt no killing blight,
Our bins are filled with goodly store.

From pestilence, fire, flood, and sword
We have been spared by thy decree,
And now with humble hearts, O Lord,
We come to pay our thanks to thee.

We feel that had our merits been
The measure of thy gifts to us,

We erring children, born of sin,
Might not now be rejoicing thus.

No deed of ours hath brought us grace;
When thou wert nigh our sight was dull,
We hid in trembling from thy face,
But thou, O God, wert merciful.

Thy mighty hand o'er all the land
Hath still been open to bestow
Those blessings which our wants demand
From heaven, whence all blessings flow.

Thou hast, with ever watchful eye,
Looked down on us with holy care,
And from thy storehouse in the sky
Hast scattered plenty everywhere.

Then lift we up our songs of praise
To thee, O Father, good and kind;
To thee we consecrate our days;
Be thine the temple of each mind.

With incense sweet our thanks ascend;
Before thy works our powers pall;
Though we should strive years without end,
We could not thank thee for them all.

Why This Prayer?

A song of thanksgiving and praise for God's blessings, this poem and prayer can apply broadly to countless circumstances in our life. Perfect to recite at a Thanksgiving dinner, it's also tuned to the daily godsends we receive—through no worth or privilege of our own. God takes pleasure in listening and honoring the requests of the children He loves, and when we look over the accounting of our lives, giving thanks for each blessing truly would take a lifetime.

72

Anna Shipton

Born in England in 1815, Anna Shipton was an English religious poet. Her first work found publication at the age of fourteen, though most of her significant poems were penned later. She published nearly two dozen volumes in England and the United States.

Are we silent to Jesus? Think! Have you nothing to ask Him? Nothing to thank Him for? Nothing to praise Him for? Nothing to confess? Oh, poor soul, go back to Bethlehem—to Gethsemane, to Calvary, and remember at what a cost the veil before the Holies was rent in twain that thou mightest enter it.

Why This Prayer?

Every beat of the New Testament is about Jesus' death and resurrection, and everything that changed in those seconds, minutes, hours, and days. Advent is about prayer. The manger is about prayer. So is the escape to Egypt and the years of learning and the calling of the disciples and the miracles and sermons. It's all about establishing this Son of Man as Son of God and giving Him the authority and power to intercede on our behalf. First for the forgiveness of our sins and then for the yearnings of our heart. Silence, in the wake of that understanding, is tantamount to sacrilege. We pray because He's waiting. Because He gave everything.

187

73

WALTER RAUSCHENBUSCH

Walter Rauschenbusch pastored the Second German Baptist Church near the Hell's Kitchen neighborhood in New York City. A graduate of Rochester Theological Seminary, Rauschenbusch began heading the church in 1885 and quickly became alert to the poverty and issues facing the area and people he served for over a decade. He became a warrior on behalf of the needs of the most vulnerable and saw the Church as the key tool for God's work on behalf of the poor and infirm. He published numerous books on the issue, including *A Theology for the Social Gospel* in 1917.

O God, we thank you for this universe, our great home; for its vast-ness and its riches, and for the abundance of the life which teems upon it and of which we are part. We praise thee for the arching sky and the blessed winds, for the driving clouds and the stars on high. We praise thee for the salt sea and the running water, for the everlasting hills, for the trees, and for the grass under our feet. We thank you for our senses by which we can see the splendor of the morning, hear the jubilant songs of love, and smell the breath of the springtime. Grant us, we pray, a heart wide open to all this joy and beauty. Save our souls from being so steeped in care or so darkened by passion that we pass heedless and unseeing when even the thorn bush by the wayside is aflame with the glory of God.

Enlarge within us the sense of fellowship with all living things, our little brothers and sisters, to whom you have given this earth as their home in common with us. May we realize that they live, not for us alone, but for themselves and for thee, and that they love the sweetness of life just as we do, and serve thee in their place. When our use of this world is over and we make room for others, may we not leave anything ravished by our greed or spoiled by our ignorance; but may we hand on our common heritage fairer and sweeter through our use of it. And then, may our bodies return in peace to mother earth who for so long nourished them. Amen.

Why This Prayer?

Have you had the opportunity this day, this week, to be inspired by Creation? God's handiwork is right outside our windows, and yet too often we overlook it. He spent five days forming the space that would become our home, and yet there are days when we barely lift our eyes from man-made screens. Rauschenbusch's prayer is not unique in its wonder of the world. In fact, it's the words we often share when Creation catches our breath. Even in the smallest of things—a house wren flitting outside or a long steady rain or the twitching of our dog's nose at dinner—we see the most inventive and playful side of God. There is joy and wonder all around us, and God is the proud maker, waiting for His efforts to be noticed.

PRAYERS *for* MERCY WHEN OUR HEARTS STRAY

Have mercy on me, O God, according to your unfailing love; according to your great compassion blot out my transgressions.

Psalm 51:1

74

DISMAS *the* GOOD THIEF

It'd be an amazing coincidence if his name actually was Dismas, but that is the moniker that time and tradition has given him through the years. What we know of him is that he was a thief and that he understood both his own guilt and that the man dying next to him was blameless. What he knew of Jesus and how he knew anything of His ministry isn't clear, but his pained request—"Remember me when you come into your kingdom"—speaks volumes. It's spoken in the same voice that all sinners—all of us—speak to God in. And how fortunate a man he was to hear the reply he received.

> *My Crucified Jesus,*
> *wash me with your most Precious Blood.*
> *Look upon me as the good thief,*
> *who hung on the cross next to You at Calvary.*
> *A sinner, paying for his crimes,*
> *but recognizes your divinity*
> *and begs for mercy and forgiveness*
> *and asks: "Jesus, remember me when you come into your*
>   *kingdom."*

Dear Lord, look upon me like the Good Thief.
And I should be so lucky, full of Peace. Amen.

———————— WHY THIS PRAYER? ————————

The big lives in the Bible—the examples of David and Peter and Paul—are full of moments of confession and forgiveness. But almost no single person mentioned in the Bible represents the exquisite wonder of grace more than this penitent thief. He's the embodiment of it. If grace required anything more, in fact, than acknowledging our desperate need for lasting mercy, the poor man would never have experienced it. He was being executed. He could not change his life around, could not earn God's favor by repaying what he stole. He could only let Jesus take the weight of his sins and then hear what could only be the most beautiful of words, "Truly I tell you, today you will be with me in paradise" (Luke 23:43).

75

JOHANN SEBASTIAN BACH

Johann Sebastian Bach was born in Germany in 1685. Music was a huge part of his upbringing, but he wasn't a childhood prodigy like other well-known composers. Instead, the music education he received as a child fed into his career as a church musician and organist. The rest of his life was spent in the service of both God and music, writing countless sacred compositions, especially for the organ and keyboard instruments to which he would be most closely tied. His major works include the *Goldberg Variations*, "Jesu, Joy of Man's Desiring," and the *St. Matthew Passion*, among many others.

> *We hasten with weak, yet eager footsteps,*
> *O Jesus, O Master, for your help alone!*
> *You tirelessly seek out the sick and those who have gone astray.*
> *Oh, hear us, as we, our voices raised, pray for your help!*
> *May your merciful countenance be gracious unto us!*

──── WHY THIS PRAYER? ────

This prayer is taken from one of more than two hundred cantatas Bach wrote; this one—BWV 78—was written specifically for the fourteenth Sunday after Trinity in the liturgical Church calendar. The specific Sunday matters less than the devotion of the man writing music not just for Holy Week or Advent but for all of the Sundays. For some, church may only be something that is two or three special services a year. For others, it might even be fifty-two services a year. But worship and prayer were never intended to be confined only to the walls of a building and the hours of a service. Bach's music and words have moved throughout history, and countless listeners have heard holy words and notes offered to God. Bach made some of the most joyful noises of any person ever, and if we can raise our voices alongside his, we can find a bit of that inspiration as well.

76

ALBRECHT DÜRER

Albrecht Dürer was a German painter during the Renaissance period. Born in 1471 and raised in a goldsmith's shop, Dürer showed early signs of artistic skill and was apprenticed to a painter and woodcut illustrator from whom he would learn his craft. Like many painters of the time, his masterworks were religious in theme, though faith was important in his life as well. His most famous works include *Praying Hands*, which hangs in the ALBERTINA Museum, Vienna, and *Adam and Eve*, part of the Metropolitan Museum of Art collection in New York City.

O God in heaven, have mercy on us! O Lord Jesus Christ, pray for thy people, redeem us in thy right time, keep us in the true Christian faith, collect thy far-separated sheep by thy voice, heard in thy Holy Word! Help us to recognize thy voice so that we may not follow any device of man's invention. And in order that we may not turn away from thee, Lord Jesus Christ, call together again the sheep of thy fold . . .

WHY THIS PRAYER?

Taken from his journal in 1521, Dürer uses what feels like a very modern phrase when he asks God's protection from "any device of man's invention." What's interesting is that he's asking for protection because of how unexpectedly appealing the world can be to us. In an increasingly hectic world, it's easy to be distracted by the noise and arguments and find ourselves overwhelmed. The still, small voice of God can be lost to the shouting . . . even if it's just the shouting of words online. We need respite and peace and to be delivered at an opportune time. Perhaps that's today for you, this moment. We are His sheep and He is our Shepherd, and when we're in need He'll be there.

77

John Newton

If you know anything of John Newton you know he wrote the hymn "Amazing Grace" and that the words stand out so power-fully—"that saved a wretch like me"—because he was a wretch of almost unfathomable depths. A captain of ships transporting enslaved men and women, Newton later became not only an ordained pastor but a prominent voice for abolition. He penned "Thoughts Upon the African Slave Trade," which detailed the horrors of his past employment and was sent to members of Parliament.

Alas! Most gracious Lord, what shall I say? I have nothing to offer for all thy goodness but new confessions of my guilt. That thou art kind to the unthankful and the evil, I am one of the most remark-able instances. Forgive me, I beseech thee, this year of misspent life, and charge me not with the long abuse of thy bounty. I owe thee ten thousand talents, and have nothing to pay. Yet I entreat thee to have patience with me—not that it will be ever in my power to make any amends by the best I can do, but because my Savior Jesus Christ, thy beloved Son, has done and suffered more than sufficient to atone for all my offenses, and to supply all my defects. Let me plead his merits on behalf of myself. . . .

—————— Why This Prayer? ——————

Who is the worst of sinners? You are. I am. We are. Paul was. 1 Timothy 1:15 offers, "Here is a trustworthy saying that deserves full acceptance: Christ Jesus came into the world to save sinners—of whom I am the worst." John Newton certainly was the worst of sinners. He felt it acutely and felt the illumination of grace perhaps all the more because of it. It's sometimes too easy to skip lightly over our confessions, too easy not to look truthfully into the mirror of our souls. There are a million people "worse" than us out there every day. And yet, there isn't a single one. No one person is more in need of grace than you. Or me. Or us. We are all fully dependent on Jesus' saving actions on our behalf, and without Him, we're all just captains of our own ships of sin.

78

John Knox

John Knox brought fists and fire to the Gospel. Born in Scotland in the early 1500s, Knox lived in a country where the Catholic Church owned more than half the land. As the Reformation made its way across to the British Isles, Knox accepted its teachings and became a bodyguard for an early Protestant preacher. Called then to be a preacher himself, Knox was eventually arrested and enslaved for a time. When he gained his freedom, he spent a number of wandering years preaching before returning to Scotland in 1555 and again in 1559. He preached with fire and ferocity, and among his writings were the *Scots Confession of 1560*, which he helped write, and *The History of the Reformation of Religion in Scotland*.

Omnipotent and everlasting God, Father of our Lord Jesus Christ, who by thy eternal providence disposest kingdoms as seemeth best to thy wisdom: we acknowledge and confess thy judgments to be righteous, in that thou hast taken from us, for our ingratitude, and for abusing of thy most holy word, our native king and earthly comforter. Justly mayest thou pour forth upon us the uttermost of thy plagues, for that we have not known the day and time of our merciful visitation. We have contemned thy word, and despised thy mercies: we have transgressed thy laws, for deceitfully have we wrought every man with our neighbor; oppression and violence we have not abhorred, charity hath not appeared among us, as our profession requireth. We have little regarded the voices of thy prophets; thy threatenings we have esteemed vanity and wind. So that in us, as of ourselves, rests nothing worthy of thy mercies, for all are found fruitless, even the princes with the prophets as withered trees, apt and meet to be burned in the fire of thy eternal displeasure.

But, O Lord, behold thy own mercy and goodness, that thou mayest purge and remove the most filthy burden of our most horrible offenses. Let thy love overcome the severity of thy judgments, even as it did in giving to the world thy only Son, Jesus, when all mankind was lost, and no obedience was left in Adam nor in his seed. Regenerate our hearts, O Lord, by the strength of the Holy Ghost: convert thou us, and we shall be converted: work thou in us unfeigned repentance, and move thou our hearts to obey thy holy laws.

Behold our troubles and apparent destruction, and stay the sword of thy vengeance before it devour us. Place above us, O Lord, for thy great mercies' sake, such a head, with such rulers and magistrates, as fear they name, and will the glory of Christ Jesus to spread. Take not from us the light of thy Evangel . . . Repress thou the pride of those that would rebel, and remove from all hearts the contempt of thy word. Let not our enemies rejoice at our destruction, but look thou to the honour of thy own name, O Lord, and let thy Gospel be preached with boldness in this realm. If thy justice must punish, then punish our bodies with the rod of thy mercy. But, O Lord, let us never revolt, nor turn back to idolatry again. Mitigate the hearts of those that persecute us, and let us not faint under the cross of our Saviour; but assist us with the Holy Ghost, even to the end.

Why This Prayer?

Some days you need a little bit of good old-fashioned fire and brimstone. Knox, five hundred years ago, knew how to offer a confession. There is power and energy in these words, and looking through Knox's prayer, you feel your pulse beat a little faster. Every verb is active; this is a prayer that's distraught at the worthlessness of a heart lost to sin and despairing of what we are at our worst. Too often we're not willing to be honest in those moments. "Forgive us our trespasses" we say, as though we've merely stepped a toe onto land that isn't ours. Our sin, everyone's sin, is a stain that nothing can clean but the bloody death of Jesus. That's how bleak it is, if we're honest. Knox speaks to that moment. Perhaps it is not for all days, but it should be for some.

79

JOHN DONNE

John Donne is best known as a poet, one of the greatest of his age. Born in London in 1572, Donne was raised Catholic in a country where they were now the minority, as Anglicanism had become the state-approved religion. Much of Donne's poetry is fueled by faith and religion and by the tension between sacred and human love. He tried to avoid being brought into the religious conflicts of the day, but eventually he was forced to take on Anglicanism. He was even denied any employment outside the Anglican church by King James I. He became dean of St. Paul's Cathedral and was much regarded throughout London for his preaching. His most famous poems include "A Valediction: Forbidding Mourning" and a few of his Holy Sonnets, such as "Batter my heart, three-person'd God" and "Death, be not proud."

> Forgive me, O Lord,
> O Lord, forgive me my sins,
> the sins of my youth,
> and my present sins,
> the sin that my parents cast upon me,

original sin,
and the sins that I cast upon my children,
in an ill example;
actual sins,
sins which are manifest to all the world,
and sins which I have so labored to hide from the world,
as that now they are hid from mine own conscience,
and mine own memory.

Forgive me my crying sins,
and my whispering sins,
sins of uncharitable hate,
and sins of unchaste love,
sins against thee and against thy power, O almighty Father,
against thy wisdom, O glorious Son,
against thy goodness, O blessed Spirit of God;
and sins against him and him,
against superiors and equals,
and inferiors;
and sins against me and me,
against mine own soul,
and against my body,
which I have loved better than my soul.

Forgive me, O Lord,
O Lord, in the merits of thy Christ and my Jesus,
thine anointed,
and my savior.

Forgive me my sins,
all my sins,
and I will put Christ to no more cost,
nor thee to more trouble,
for any reprobation or malediction that lay upon me,
otherwise than as a sinner.
Amen.

——————— WHY THIS PRAYER? ———————

Which sin is it today? Donne knows the human heart, knows all the ways in which it is possible for us to sin, and the myriad of people against whom we falter. It is perhaps unlikely that every day needs this laundry list, but it is completely true that every day needs a piece of this list. So, which is it today? A sin of love, of hate? Against your superior, your inferior? Sins still weighing us down from years past, or those committed even seconds ago? They all can and must be laid at the feet of God. And they will be forgiven. And then tomorrow the humbling, wondrous act will work itself through again, and then again, and then again, for we are nothing otherwise, than sinners all.

80

St. Augustine

Augustine of Hippo is the author of *The City of God* and *Confessions*, among other works. His influence as a theologian and philosopher on Western Christianity is enormous, and he is considered a saint in the Catholic Church. Augustine's early life, however, was not devout, and it was only after a somewhat later conversion that Augustine turned his sharp mind to the Church and theology. He became the bishop of Hippo, a city in what is now Algeria, in 395 or 396 and remained in the position until his death. Despite the dissolution of the Roman Empire and the conquest of Hippo, Augustine's writings survived and became critical texts for the Church.

For your mercies' sake, O Lord my God, tell me what You are to me. Say to my soul: "I am your salvation." So speak that I may hear, O Lord; my heart is listening; open it that it may hear You, and say to my soul: "I am your salvation." After hearing this word, may I come in haste to take hold of you. Hide not Your face from me. Let me see Your face even if I die, lest I die with longing to see it. The house of my soul is too small to receive You; let it be enlarged by You. It is all in ruins; do You repair it. There are things in it, I confess and I know, that must offend Your sight. But who shall cleanse it? Or to what others besides You shall I cry out? From my secret sins cleanse me, O Lord, and from those of others spare your servant. Amen.

Why This Prayer?

It is not surprising that a man known for his *Confessions* speaks so eloquently and interestingly on the topic. If the soul can be compared to a house—with the Spirit indwelling—what care do we take with it? We know how we live and decorate and maintain other spaces. How does it compare with our efforts at sustaining and maintaining our souls? And in the end, how often do we recognize that the shape of our soul is actually in God's hand? We must look to God as landlord and owner, for we are impermanent tenants in this world who should be grateful and mindful of what we've been given to tend.

81

VICTOR HUGO

Victor Hugo is a French novelist who penned *Les Misérables* and *The Hunchback of Notre-Dame*, along with numerous other novels, plays, and poems. Hugo was immersed in French culture and politics, and in 1851, he fled the country after opposing Napoleon III, whose coup launched France's Second Empire. Hugo lived in exile for nearly twenty years, and during this time he completed his masterwork *Les Misérables*. Though separated for most of his life from the Catholic Church in which he was raised, Hugo prayed daily and sought eternal answers to the hard questions of life.

> *For our part, adjourning the development of our thought to another occasion, we will confine ourselves to saying that we neither understand man as a point of departure nor progress as an end, without those two forces which are their two motors: faith and love.*
>
> *Progress is the goal, the ideal is the type.*
> *What is this ideal? It is God.*
> *Ideal, absolute, perfection, infinity: identical words.*

WHY THIS PRAYER?

The prayer most often associated with *Les Misérables*—which Jean Valjean offers over a wounded Marius—does not appear verbatim in the novel but was written specifically for the musical. *"If I die, let me die,"* he prays. *"Let him live."* Valjean is one of the most notable recipients of grace in all of literature, and *Les Misérables* is a deeply spiritual (and massive) book in which there are often philosophical and religious musings that can't help but seem to emerge from Hugo himself. The above is not a traditional prayer, but it serves as a focus for our thoughts on the highest of things, which too many voices of the time were saying did not exist. Praying in the absence of a true north, lifting words to something less than the ideal, less than absolute, less than infinity, is folly. It's only in acknowledging perfection and being driven by faith and love that we move forward in life. All else is foundering.

82

CHARLES D'ARCY

Charles D'Arcy studied at Trinity College in Dublin, where he eventually earned his Doctor of Divinity in 1900. He served in numerous roles in the church, including Archbishop of Dublin and Archbishop of Armagh. He wrote numerous articles and books on theology, and his autobiography was titled *The Adventures of a Bishop: A Phase in Irish Life.*

Have mercy, O God, on our distracted and suffering world, on the nations perplexed and divided. Give to us and to all people a new spirit of repentance and amendment; direct the counsels of all who are working for the removal of the causes of strife and for the promotion of goodwill; and hasten the coming of thy kingdom of peace and love; through Jesus Christ our Lord.

WHY THIS PRAYER?

So often, historic prayers a hundred or even multiple hundreds of years old still sound modern to our ears, if not in the words used, then in the emotions and needs conveyed. Our world has not become any less distracted, nor offered much less suffering, since D'Arcy lifted his prayer. We are perplexed and more divided than ever, even within nations. The call, as always, for followers of God is to repentance. It is an acknowledgment that the work of hastening the coming of a kingdom of peace and love begins with humility in each of us. It is a place we so rarely start—but it is the only first step that matters.

PRAYERS
for DAILY
FAITHFULNESS

Be joyful in hope, patient in affliction, faithful in prayer.

Romans 12:12

83

The LORD'S PRAYER

We know how Jesus, when asked by His disciples how they should pray, answered. But when did the prayer become a fixture of church services? Nailing down a precise date on that is impossible. Given the importance of oral tradition in the early Church, it's almost certain that the words of the Lord's Prayer were spoken almost immediately among believers. We do have record of St. Cyprian, an early church father, writing an entire treatise between 246 and 258 that highlights how critically important the prayer is for believers.

> *Our Father which art in heaven,*
> *Hallowed be thy name.*
> *Thy kingdom come,*
> *Thy will be done in earth,*
> *as it is in heaven.*
> *Give us this day our daily bread.*
> *And forgive us our debts, as we forgive our debtors.*
> *And lead us not into temptation, but deliver us from evil:*
> *For thine is the kingdom, and the power, and the glory, for*
>   *ever.*
> *Amen.*

WHY THIS PRAYER?

This is likely the most prayed prayer in Church history. It's the archetype of all prayers—concise and compact and yet a model for all the kinds of words we can lift to God. Words of adoration and worship. Pleas for mercy and forgiveness. Humble requests for guidance and the needs of life. Deep and abiding offerings of thanks for every way God works in our lives. Believers have been reciting it—in some form—for hundreds of years. And whether you say *debts* or *trespasses* or *sins*—sometimes accidentally using the alternate phrase in another church!—it's the foundational prayer upon which all others are built. Whether you say it every week, recite it communally, sing it using the melody of Albert Hay Malotte, or simply repeat it in silence as you read again through Scripture, it's an echo of history and faith that has rung through time.

84

JANE AUSTEN

The author of *Pride and Prejudice*, *Sense and Sensibility*, and *Emma*, among other renowned novels, Jane Austen had a literary brilliance matched by few in the English language. Her wit was paired with a keen eye for uncovering the raw emotions and deep passions underlying the otherwise restrained Regency life. She was particularly sensitive to the difficulties faced by women and the plight of the less fortunate—and offered sharp critiques of the hypocrisy to be found among some of those in power, whether that be in the Church, the government, or just among the wealthy gentry.

Father of Heaven! whose goodness has brought us in safety to the close of this day, dispose our hearts in fervent prayer. Another day is now gone, and added to those, for which we were before accountable. Teach us almighty father, to consider this solemn truth, as we should do, that we may feel the importance of every day, and every hour as it passes, and earnestly strive to make a better use of what thy goodness may yet bestow on us, than we have done of the time past. Give us grace to endeavour after a truly Christian spirit to seek to attain that temper of forbearance and patience of which our blessed saviour has set us the highest example; and which, while it prepares us for the spiritual happiness of the life to come, will secure to us the best enjoyment of what this world can give. Incline us oh God! to think humbly of ourselves, to be severe only in the examination of our own conduct, to consider our fellow-creatures with kindness, and to judge of all they say and do with that charity which we would desire from them ourselves. We thank thee with all our hearts for every gracious dispensation, for all the blessings that have attended our lives, for every hour of safety, health and peace, of domestic comfort and in-nocent enjoyment. We feel that we have been blessed far beyond any thing that we have deserved; and though we cannot but pray for a continuance of all these mercies, we acknowledge our unworthiness of them and implore thee to pardon the presumption of our desires. Keep us oh! Heavenly Father from evil this night. Bring us in safety to the beginning of another day and grant that we may rise again with every serious and religious feeling which now directs us. May thy mercy be extended over all mankind, bringing the ignorant to the knowledge of thy truth, awakening the impenitent, touching the hardened. Look with compassion upon the afflicted of every condi-tion, assuage the pangs of disease, comfort the broken in spirit. More particularly do we pray for the safety and welfare of our own family and friends wheresoever dispersed, beseeching thee to avert from them all material and lasting evil of body or mind; and may we by the as-sistance of thy holy spirit so conduct ourselves on earth as to secure an eternity of happiness with each other in thy heavenly kingdom. Grant this most merciful Father, for the sake of our blessed saviour in whose holy name and words we further address thee. . . .

—— WHY THIS PRAYER? ——

Austen's books are not overt in espousing messages of faith, but they are thematically rich as she champions mercy and kindness, joy and goodness, and many other fruits of the Spirit. We know where Jane was baptized and where she and her family attended church regularly, St. Nicholas Church in Steventon, and we know that she authored at least three prayers in her life, this being one of them. Her character Fanny in *Mansfield Park* laments that daily prayer is no longer a part of regular life, saying, "There is something in a chapel and chaplain so much in character with a great house, with one's ideas of what such a household should be! A whole family assembling regularly for the purpose of prayer is fine!" Jane and her family practiced daily evening prayers, and you can imagine the prayer above being read aloud one evening. It is perhaps not an easy thing to think about being held accountable for every minute, every hour, every day, and yet she asks for God's reminder that we *must* think that way. And we must also turn to Him both in thanks for the mercy that covers over the hours when we have failed, and in gratitude when we can take on even a bit of His Spirit as we step into a new day.

85

HARRIET BEECHER STOWE

Harriet Beecher Stowe is known primarily for writing *Uncle Tom's Cabin*, though she published numerous books in her lifetime, including other novels, scripts, memoirs, and poetry. *Uncle Tom's Cabin* was a publishing phenomenon, both in the United States and even in England, where it helped fuel the growing anti-slavery movement. A dramatic version packed houses. Stowe's work wasn't her only effort on behalf of abolition, though; her family was involved with the Underground Railroad and helped slaves on their way to Canada.

> *Abide in me; there have been moments blest*
> *When I have heard Thy voice and felt Thy power;*
> *Then evil lost its grasp, and passion hushed,*
> *Owned the divine enchantment of the hour.*
>
> *These were but seasons, beautiful and rare;*
> *Abide in me and they shall ever be;*
> *Fulfil at once Thy precept and my prayer;*
> *Come, and abide in me, and I in Thee.*

─────── Why This Prayer? ───────

Stowe was the bestselling author of her time after *Uncle Tom's Cabin*. She's become synonymous with the novel—a work that has undergone various critiques throughout the years—to a degree that it does her a disservice. Her true heart was with the Church, and while her faith fueled her passion for abolition, it wasn't the whole of her. This prayer, written as a hymn by Stowe, is another glance into her heart. Writing of those seasons when God felt most near, "beautiful and rare," she puts to paper what is so often in our hearts when we pray. *Draw close, God. Closer. Closer and never leave.*

86

St. Thérèse
of Lisieux

Born Marie-Françoise-Thérèse Martin in 1873, Thérèse of Lisieux was a French nun who eventually was named a Doctor of the Church because of the importance of her writings, including her autobiography, *Story of a Soul*. She gained the nickname "Little Flower" because of her love of flowers and believed that, like flowers, she could most glorify God by living a simple, beautiful life. She died at the age of twenty-four.

> *O my God! I offer Thee all my actions of this day for the intentions and for the glory of the Sacred Heart of Jesus. I desire to sanctify every beat of my heart, my every thought, my simplest works, by uniting them to Its infinite merits; and I wish to make reparation for my sins by casting them into the furnace of Its Merciful Love.*
>
> *O my God! I ask of Thee for myself and for those whom I hold dear, the grace to fulfill perfectly Thy Holy Will, to accept for love of Thee the joys and sorrows of this passing life, so that we may one day be united together in heaven for all Eternity. Amen.*

─────── **WHY THIS PRAYER?** ───────

It should not be surprising that many of the prayers in this book emerged from the hearts of pastors and nuns and monks and missionaries. These people devoted their lives—and most of their thoughts—to spiritual matters. While it's likely that a landscaper or mason or coder has offered a particularly eloquent prayer to God, they're often not focused on writing them down, and their very days aren't built around meditating on God's love. We all need, though, a little bit of that contemplation, or we risk focusing on our own private concerns from day to day. A morning prayer, like the one above, is an ideal place to start because it begins each morning with the prayer version of an alarm clock. The challenge to let God sanctify every heartbeat is a request for Him to intrude and guide our lives and steps in every way.

87

GEORGE MACDONALD

George MacDonald is one of those rare people who is most well-known for being beloved by an even more famous person. C. S. Lewis devoured the works of MacDonald, particularly *Phantastes*, and counted the Scottish author—who wrote across a number of genres, including poetry, fantasy, and Highland romances—as a major influence on his own works, including appearing in Lewis's *The Great Divorce*. MacDonald was born in Scotland in 1824 and spent time as both a minister and professor.

Am I going out into the business and turmoil of the day, where so many temptations may come to do less honourably, less faithfully, less kindly, less diligently than the Ideal Man would have me do?—Father, into thy hands. Am I going to do a good deed? Then, of all times,—Father, into thy hands; lest the enemy should have me now. Am I going to do a hard duty, from which I would gladly be turned aside,—to refuse a friend's request, to urge a neighbour's conscience?—Father, into thy hands I commend my spirit. Am I in pain? Is illness coming upon me to shut out the glad visions of a healthy brain, and bring me such as are troubled and untrue?—Take my spirit, Lord, and see, as thou art wont, that it has no more to bear than it can bear. Am I going to die? . . . Father, into thy hands I commend my spirit. For it is thy business, not mine. Thou wilt know every shade of my suffering; thou wilt care for me with thy perfect fatherhood. . . .

—————— WHY THIS PRAYER? ——————

No morning prayer can capture all the endless possibilities that a person at dawn faces. Though many times it feels like our days feel repetitive, with little surprise, in truth, each day does offer endless possibilities, and MacDonald seeks to at least hint at the enormity of that. And he knows that in each and every circumstance, imagined or not, God will care for him, for us.

88

ST. PATRICK

If we know anything of St. Patrick, it is that he ministered in Ireland and that somehow a holiday celebrating his death on March 17 has turned into a tumult of green and alcohol. In history, St. Patrick lived during the early fifth century and was instrumental as a missionary to the island of Ireland. He first spent a number of years imprisoned on the island after being taken in by Irish pirates, returning after a vision from God pointed him to head back. Tradition holds that he helped drive all the snakes from Ireland as well, but that is more legend than fact.

> *I arise today*
> *Through a mighty strength, the invocation of the Trinity,*
> *Through a belief in the Threeness,*
> *Through confession of the Oneness*
> *Of the Creator of creation.*
> *I arise today*
> *Through the strength of Christ's birth and His baptism,*
> *Through the strength of His crucifixion and His burial,*
> *Through the strength of His resurrection and His ascension,*
> *Through the strength of His descent for the judgment of doom.*
> *I arise today*

Through the strength of the love of cherubim,
In obedience of angels,
In service of archangels,
In the hope of resurrection to meet with reward,
In the prayers of patriarchs,
In preachings of the apostles,
In faiths of confessors,
In innocence of virgins,
In deeds of righteous men.
I arise today
Through the strength of heaven;
Light of the sun,
Splendor of fire,
Speed of lightning,
Swiftness of the wind,
Depth of the sea,
Stability of the earth,
Firmness of the rock.
I arise today
Through God's strength to pilot me;
God's might to uphold me,
God's wisdom to guide me,
God's eye to look before me,
God's ear to hear me,
God's word to speak for me,
God's hand to guard me,
God's way to lie before me,
God's shield to protect me,
God's hosts to save me
From snares of the devil,
From temptations of vices,
From every one who desires me ill,
Afar and anear,
Alone or in a multitude.
I summon today all these powers between me and evil,

Against every cruel merciless power that opposes my body and
    soul,
Against incantations of false prophets,
Against black laws of pagandom,
Against false laws of heretics,
Against craft of idolatry,
Against spells of women and smiths and wizards,
Against every knowledge that corrupts man's body and soul.
Christ shield me today
Against poison, against burning,
Against drowning, against wounding,
So that reward may come to me in abundance.
Christ with me, Christ before me, Christ behind me,
Christ in me, Christ beneath me, Christ above me,
Christ on my right, Christ on my left,
Christ when I lie down, Christ when I sit down,
Christ in the heart of every man who thinks of me,
Christ in the mouth of every man who speaks of me,
Christ in the eye that sees me,
Christ in the ear that hears me.
I arise today
Through a mighty strength, the invocation of the Trinity,
Through a belief in the Threeness,
Through a confession of the Oneness
Of the Creator of creation.

--------------------- **WHY THIS PRAYER?** ---------------------

The prepositional portion of this prayer—"Christ in me, Christ before me, Christ behind me . . ."—is one of the most famous in the world and comes from a larger morning prayer that has long been attributed to St. Patrick and is often known as "St. Patrick's Breastplate." In the Bible, Ephesians 6 describes the armor of God and includes the breastplate of righteousness, which is the piece that shields the heart. The prayer walks us through a solemn moment in which we begin a process of right thinking for the day that will hopefully carry over, in Christ's strength, into right living. A breastplate is not a comfortable or easy piece of armor to be worn. This prayer is a fine way to go about the work of daily fitting it onto our lives for its intended purpose.

89

SUSANNA WESLEY

Though she was born and died in England, Susanna Wesley's influence on faith and religion in the United States and the world is often understated. In another time and era she could have been a well-known Bible teacher herself. Born in 1669, though, she had limited roles available to her, and yet God still moved through her in powerful ways. She was the mother of John and Charles Wesley, and their upbringing under her care shaped them into the men they became. Her writings included commentaries and devotionals, all meant for private family use rather than publishing glory, yet many still survive, as does her legacy as the "Mother of Methodism."

> You, O Lord, have called us to watch and pray.
> Therefore, whatever may be the sin against which we pray,
> make us careful to watch against it,
> and so have reason to expect that our prayers will be answered.
> In order to perform this duty aright,
> grant us grace to preserve a sober, equal temper,
> and sincerity to pray for your assistance. Amen.

———— WHY THIS PRAYER? ————

Susanna Wesley delivered nineteen children, though nine did not live past infancy. Her husband, Samuel, a minister, struggled often with money and found himself in jail at times for his debts. Susanna Wesley is looked on as a paragon of faith, but her life was never easy. Still, filled with the love and guidance of God, she created a home that produced two of the most influential church leaders of the eighteenth century. Tradition holds that Susanna's home was often so busy that she could not easily carve out space for prayer. Instead, she pulled her apron over her head and instructed her children that time was sacred because it was time she was spending in communion with God. A prayer about the importance of praying may seem redundant, but in a cluttered and hectic life, perhaps calling out to God for the peace and space to engage with Him fully is more needed than we might want to admit.

90

FRED ROGERS

Fred Rogers—"Mister Rogers," as he was better known to millions of children and parents—hosted a warm and inviting kids public television show for more than thirty years. Rogers began *Mister Rogers' Neighborhood* for WQED out of Pittsburgh in 1968 after years of working behind the scenes on other children's programming. He hosted nearly nine hundred episodes of the educational program. Rogers was also an ordained Presbyterian minister.

Dear God, let some word that is heard be Yours.

——————— WHY THIS PRAYER? ———————

Fred Rogers told a reporter that this was the prayer he offered before every program. He knew that the show he was working on reached millions of young eyes over the entire country. He also knew it wasn't specifically a religious show, though it was filled with themes and examples of the fruit of the Spirit. Love, joy, peace, forbearance, kindness, goodness, faithfulness, gentleness, and self-control all were spoken of and presented as traits every child should strive to achieve. We are not able to preach in every moment of our lives, but we can live God's love—and we can pray also that in the words that come from our lips, one might be heard as His.

91

GEORGE MÜLLER

George Müller was a nineteenth century English evangelist and missionary whose name has become nearly synonymous with the power—and persistence—of prayer. The phrase "prayer warrior" likely didn't exist in his day, but if it did, he would have worn that mantle easily. Müller helped establish and run the Ashley Down orphanage in Bristol, which at its height helped house more than two thousand children.

> *Lord Jesus, Thou hast the same power now. Thou canst provide me with means for Thy work in my hands. Be pleased to do so.*

WHY THIS PRAYER?

The costs of building and running the five homes that made up the Ashley Down orphanage were enormous, and yet George Müller never solicited funds. He trusted in faith, prayed constantly, and the needs of the ministry were met, sometimes in miraculous fashion. The prayer above was spoken in 1852, according to his journal. It was a somewhat dire financial time, and Müller was reading about Jesus healing the centurion's servant and raising the widow of Nain's son from the dead—surely a little debt was nothing compared to death. Within thirty minutes of praying, unexpected donations arrived, and the ministry moved forward. Sometimes the answers to our prayers are just that quick, just that clear. Sometimes God is pleased to meet us exactly where and when we pray, sometimes even while we're still on our knees. He has the power; He always has. We need the diligence to go to Him in prayer.

PRAYERS
for HUMILITY

He guides the humble in what is right and teaches them his way.

Psalm 25:9

92

JULIAN *of* NORWICH

Revelations of Divine Love is the oldest surviving book that was written by a woman in the English language. The book was written in the late 1300s and finally was published for the first time in 1670. Julian of Norwich chose to live primarily in seclusion, an anchoress in a cell attached to St. Julian's Church in Norwich, England. There she wrote and prayed and prayed and wrote, and her manuscripts—descriptions of visions she had, divine encounters with the holy—survived centuries.

> *God, of your goodness, give me yourself; you are enough for me, and anything less that I could ask for would not do you full honor. And if I ask anything that is less, I shall always lack something, but in you alone I have everything.*

—— WHY THIS PRAYER? ——

This is the prayer of an ascetic, one who strips their life down to the bare minimum. It is a life few of us would choose, a life that God calls few to. But it is the logical end for belief in a God who is our all. It would be a daunting task to list the things that sometimes get in the way of our faith, the things that keep us from making God our all, but if we dare to be honest, it's a worthy task now and then. And any time we move something from our list of supposed "needs" to our more honest list of "wants," the closer we are to taking the step that Julian of Norwich took six hundred years ago, when God was her everything.

93

GEORGE H. W. BUSH

George Herbert Walker Bush served as the forty-first president of the United States, his election coming after spending eight years as vice president with Ronald Reagan. Bush's political career was widely varied, with time spent as ambassador to the United Nations and director of the CIA being two titles on his résumé. During his four-year term, the Cold War ended with the breakup of the Soviet Union and the country entered the First Gulf War against Iraq after the invasion of Kuwait.

Heavenly Father, we bow our heads and thank You for Your love. Accept our thanks for the peace that yields this day and the shared faith that makes its continuance likely. Make us strong to do Your work, willing to heed and hear Your will, and write on our hearts these words: "Use power to help people." For we are given power not to advance our own purposes, nor to make a great show in the world, nor a name. There is but one just use of power, and it is to serve people. Help us to remember it, Lord. Amen.

——— WHY THIS PRAYER? ———

Bush's words come from his inaugural address on January 20, 1989. "There is but one just use of power, and it is to serve people.

Help us to remember it, Lord." This thought shows a humility for the position of president of the United States that is admirable. Though the words may be easier to say than act out, especially in a country where few can agree on any topic, they seem a necessary starting point—not just for civil servants in politics but in any position of power.

94

Helen Hunt Jackson

Helen Hunt Jackson was a powerful voice on behalf of Native Americans, and she became one of the first advocates to shine a light on the broken treaties and terrible treatment of Native people by the US government. She also was a poet and novelist, and her book *Ramona*, written in 1884, illustrated their mistreatment in California following the end of the Mexican-American War.

> *Father, I scarcely dare to pray,*
> *So clear I see, now it is done,*
> *That I have wasted half my day,*
> *And left my work but just begun;*
>
> *So clear I see that things I thought*
> *Were right or harmless were a sin;*
> *So clear I see that I have sought,*
> *Unconscious, selfish aims to win;*
>
> *So clear I see that I have hurt*
> *The souls I might have helped to save;*
> *That I have slothful been, inert,*
> *Deaf to the calls thy leaders gave.*

In outskirts of thy kingdoms vast,
Father, the humblest spot give me;
Set me the lowliest task thou hast;
Let me repentant work for thee!

—— Why This Prayer? ——

This is a prayer of confession and humility that urges us to be honest about the time we've spent in our day, our week, our month, our life. It's about opening our eyes to all the work to be done on God's behalf and asking ourselves if we've really given our all to it. It's about daring to see outside ourselves—see when we hurt others unintentionally or when our aims have been motivated by something other than following God's urging. It is a hard prayer, but the kind we need to offer more than just now and then. We know the Bible is full of imagery of blind eyes being given light for the first time, and it's usually presented as a good thing. Jackson here nudges us to remember that light gives us the chance to see everything—good and bad. We can't take one and just ignore the other. God, give us that light as a gift.

95

CLEMENT *of* ROME

Pope Clement I was one of the earliest bishops of Rome in history. He served in the role from around 88 to 99 and is considered the first Apostolic Father of the Church, among Polycarp, Ignatius, and others. A letter he wrote to the church in Corinth survives and is among the earliest Church writings after the Bible. Tradition claims Pope Clement was eventually martyred by drowning under Emperor Trajan.

To our rulers and governors on the earth—to them Thou, Lord, gavest the power of the kingdom by Thy glorious and ineffable might, to the end that we may know the glory and honour given to them by Thee and be subject to them, in nought resisting Thy will; to them, Lord, give health, peace, concord, stability, that they may exercise the authority given to them without offence. For Thou, O heavenly Lord and King eternal, givest to the sons of men glory and honour and power over the things that are on the earth; do Thou, Lord, direct their counsel according to that which is good and well-pleasing in Thy sight, that, devoutly in peace and meekness exercising the power given them by Thee, they may find Thee propitious. O Thou, who only hast power to do these things and more abundant good with us, we praise Thee through the High Priest and Guardian of our souls Jesus Christ,

*through whom be glory and majesty to Thee both now and from gen-
eration to generation and for evermore. Amen.*

────── WHY THIS PRAYER? ──────

Taken from Pope Clement I's epistle to the church in Corinth, the
letter shows that from even the earliest days of the Church—and
from the very start of human society—we have struggled with
leadership. There are good leaders and bad leaders; the Bible
is full of kings who followed God and kings who defied Him.
Written at a time when ordinary citizens had no role in choosing
who ruled them, they were left to pray for those who led. We
today have more voice, and while our choices may not always
be the ones elected, we are called to pray for *all* who end up in
positions of power. Our prayer is that they will follow God—not
enact a law we want or affect the economy in a way that benefits
us—and be led with humility so that God can lead through them.

96

PHILLIS WHEATLEY

In 1773, Phillis Wheatley published the volume *Poems on Various Subjects, Religious and Moral*. Not only was she among the first women to be published in the colonies, she was the first African American to publish a book. Brought to the states as a child after being kidnapped from her home in Senegal, West Africa, she was bought by John Wheatley in Boston to be a servant for his wife. The family noted her quick mind and educated Phillis, and she soon began writing. She published her first poem as a teenager and then her book of poems six years later, many of which tackled issues of faith. She was freed from slavery after the publication of her book, but the remainder of her life was marked by hard times and struggle.

> *Oh my Gracious Preserver!*
> *hitehero thou hast brot [me,]*
> *be pleased when thou bringest*
> *to the birth to give [me] strength*
> *to bring forth living & perfect a*
> *being who shall be greatly in-*
> *strumental in promoting thy [glory]*
> *Tho conceived in Sin & brot forth*
> *in iniquity yet thy infinite wisdom*

can bring a clean thing out of an
unclean, a vess[el] of Honor filled
for thy glory—grant me
to live a life of gratitude to thee
for the innumerable benefits—
O Lord my God! instruct my ignorance
& enlighten my Darkness
Thou art my King, take [thou]
the entire possession of [all] my
powers & faculties & let me be
no longer under the dominion
of sin—Give me a sincere &
hearty repentance for all my
[grievous?] offences & strengthen
by thy grace my resolutions
on amendment & circumspection
for the time to come—Grant me
[also] the spirit of Prayer & Suppli[cation]
according to thy own
most gracious Promises.

WHY THIS PRAYER?

Phillis Wheatley lived a life we cannot fathom. A million discussions can emerge from the circumstances of her life, but these will be rife with supposition and inference and guessing. We'll never have the opportunity to know the real heart of Phillis Wheatley, though her poems may give us the closest glimpse. In this poem and prayer, she offers a bended knee and contrite heart, asking for a sincere and hearty repentance. Asking God to help us repent sincerely may seem like a contradiction or an oxymoron, but in all things our spirits can be shaped and taught by God's leading.

97

Elizabeth Fry

Prisons and asylums and workhouses of the 1800s offered some of the most grave and awful conditions on earth. Elizabeth Fry, a Quaker woman with a burning passion to see change enacted, was a powerful voice of reform and rehabilitation. Among the numerous changes for which she advocated were separating inmates by gender, assigning women to oversee female prisoners, and providing useful employment to those incarcerated. Fry also helped set up a homeless shelter for London's countless destitute. Her charity and kindness gained wide attention, and she appeared before Queen Victoria numerous times.

Oh! may I be directed what to do, and what to leave undone, and then I may humbly trust, that a blessing will be with me in my various engagements. . . . At home and abroad, enable me also, O Lord! to feel tenderly and charitably towards all my beloved fellow-mortals, that I may have no soreness, nor improper feeling towards any; thinking no evil, bearing all things, hoping all things, enduring all things, that I may walk in all humility and godly fear, before all men, and in Thy sight. Amen.

——————— WHY THIS PRAYER? ———————

With the life that Elizabeth Fry lived, this prayer is like gaining practical wisdom from a genius in the field. After a visit to Newgate Prison, Fry felt called to make a difference. All of us need to open ourselves to similar nudges from the Spirit. They might not impact our lives as dramatically, so that we become devoted activists, but God wants us to be ready for His leading. It is too easy to sink into cynicism and inertia sometimes. Change, for whatever weighs on our heart, can come—through our donations of time and energy and imagination.

98

JEREMY TAYLOR

There are countless reasons why the separation of church and state is a good idea. For pastors and priests, one of the key reasons is that if the government changes, you don't lose your job—or, in centuries past, your life. Jeremy Taylor was an eloquent writer, the "Shakespeare of the Divines" as he became known, and because of his connection with Archbishop of Canterbury William Laud, he was appointed chaplain in ordinary for King Charles I. In the following years, Charles faced resistance, Taylor was imprisoned more than once, and Laud was executed. Taylor would later become chaplain to the Earl of Carbery and used this time to pen a number of works, including *The Rule and Exercises of Holy Living* and *The Rules and Exercises of Holy Dying*, which were held in esteem by John Wesley.

Guide me, O Lord, in all the changes and varieties of the world; that in all things that shall happen I may have an evenness and tranquility of spirit; that my soul may be wholly resigned to thy divine will and pleasure, never murmuring at thy gentle chastisements and fatherly correction; never waxing proud and insolent, though I feel a torrent of comforts and prosperous successes.

—— Why This Prayer? ——

Much of the life of faith is a tug-of-war between our stubborn sin nature and the ability to submit to and be led by God. This can be in the smallest of things—a gesture or even a single word—or it can be in major decisions for our life. The spirit of our age is disquiet, with greater and greater numbers of men and women acknowledging struggles with anxiety, depression, and other mental health disorders. Faith in God is not a cure-all guaranteed to rid us of those concerns. It is an unchanging bulwark, though, an anchor and guideline, to which we can hold fast during tumult. The storms in life will still toss us, but hopefully we can find some tranquility of spirit and comfort in knowing that we are still tied to something unbreakable.

99

John Wesley

John Wesley led an enormously influential life. He and his brother Charles, along with George Whitefield, helped forge the Methodist denomination of Protestantism, which became influential the world over. Born in 1703, Wesley went on to study at Oxford and became a deacon in order to pursue his graduate religious education. At Oxford, he and his brother founded the "holy club," a small group devoted to the study and practice of a devout religious life. Following a tumultuous journey to the colonies that included a harrowing storm, Wesley returned to England shaken and unsure what would come next. The Spirit found him at a Moravian service in 1738, and soon Wesley refocused on the theology and preaching that would direct his career and shape the understanding of God all over the globe.

I am no longer my own, but thine.
Put me to what thou wilt, rank me with whom thou wilt.
Put me to doing, put me to suffering.
Let me be employed by thee or laid aside for thee,
exalted for thee or brought low for thee.
Let me be full, let me be empty.
Let me have all things, let me have nothing.

I freely and heartily yield all things
to thy pleasure and disposal.
And now, O glorious and blessed God,
Father, Son, and Holy Spirit,
thou art mine, and I am thine. So be it.
And the covenant which I have made on earth,
let it be ratified in heaven. Amen.

WHY THIS PRAYER?

In the midst of our daily prayers, sometimes it's important to think back to what our first heart-and-soul prayer was as a believer. Not the prayers we recited as children, but the first one we offered on our own. This is not John Wesley's first heart-and-soul prayer—but it sounds like it could be. He continued to live with that spirit and faith, and it's instructional to us that sometimes it's worth trying to recapture those first feelings of belief when God's love seemed so new and large. Too often we try to narrow God's possibilities for us into a box of our own making rather than trusting Him with the immensity of possibilities. Do we trust Him to watch over us in sickness and unemployment and in loneliness and suffering and all the other hard times? Or do we only demand comfort and blessings?

100

Leo Tolstoy

One of the greatest novelists in the world, Tolstoy was born into Russian aristocracy in 1828. Before taking on the major works that would cement his name, he lived a more lax and unfettered life as a university student, which led to significant gambling debts. Entering the army as an escape, he served during the Crimean War. He came away from the experience changed, and it was foundational in feeding the creative fire that completed *War and Peace*. He is also known for *The Death of Ivan Ilych* and *Anna Karenina*, among other works. His spiritual autobiography, *A Confession*, details his radical awakening to Jesus' teachings.

Three are ye, three are we, have mercy upon us!

——— Why This Prayer? ———

Taken from a very short story published by Tolstoy in 1886, the prayer is one made by three hermits on a remote island. A bishop, learning of their existence, chooses to visit them. When he inquires after their spiritual practices, how they interact with God, they claim this is the only prayer they know. The bishop spends hours instructing them in the ways of prayer, giving them more elaborate and powerful words to recite, convinced that he's saving their lives, but when he boards his boat to leave that evening, the hermits rush out of the dark, terrified. They've forgotten the words he's taught them and now have nothing to offer. The bishop realizes his mistake and honors their simple faith, saying, "Your own prayer will reach the Lord, men of God. It is not for me to teach you. Pray for us sinners." The parable is simple, and paradoxical, perhaps, in a book of one hundred prayers worth knowing. Its essence, though, is about honesty and authenticity. Whatever words you use, you must own them, feel them, and bring them to God. Whether the simplest of graces or an ornate and meandering plea on your knees, honest words will find God's ear.

SOME ADVICE
on PRAYER

GEORGE MÜLLER

George Müller certainly spent more time praying than ever writing down his prayers, and most of his writings are about prayer and its power rather than words of prayer themselves. Still, he offers wisdom as we strive to make prayer a conversation rather than just words being shouted into the void.

1. I seek at the beginning to get my heart into such a state that it has no will of its own in regard to a given matter.

Nine-tenths of the trouble with people is just here. Nine-tenths of the difficulties are overcome when our hearts are ready to do the Lord's will, whatever it may be. When one is truly in this state, it is usually but a little way to the knowledge of what His will is.

2. Having done this, I do not leave the result to feeling or simple impression. If I do so, I make myself liable to great delusions.

3. I seek the will of the Spirit of God through, or in connection with, the Word of God.

The Spirit and the Word must be combined. If I look to the Spirit alone without the Word, I lay myself open to great delusions also. If the Holy Ghost guides us at all, He will do it according to the Scriptures and never contrary to them.

4. Next I take into account providential circumstances. These often plainly indicate God's will in connection with His Word and Spirit.

5. I ask God in prayer to reveal His will to me aright.

6. Thus, through prayer to God, the study of the Word, and reflection, I come to a deliberate judgment according to the best of my ability and knowledge, and if my mind is thus at peace, and continues so after two or three more petitions, I proceed accordingly.

In trivial matters, and in transactions involving most important issues, I have found this method always effective.

JOHN BUNYAN

Before you enter into prayer, ask thy soul these questions: To what end, O my soul, art thou retired into this place? Art thou not come to discourse the Lord in prayer? Is he present; will he hear thee? Is he merciful; will he help thee? Is thy business slight; is it not concerning the welfare of thy soul? What words wilt thou use to move him to compassion? To make thy preparation complete, consider that thou art but dust and ashes, and he the great God, Father of our Lord Jesus Christ, that clothes himself with light, as with a garment; that thou art a vile sinner, he a holy God; that thou art but a poor crawling worm, he the omnipotent Creator. In all your prayers forget not to thank the Lord for his mercies. When thou prayest, rather let thy heart be without words, than thy words without a heart. Prayer will make a man cease from sin, or sin will entice a man to cease from prayer.

JOHN NEWTON

I sometimes think that the prayers of believers afford a stronger proof of a depraved nature, than even the profaneness of those who know not the Lord. How strange is it, that when I have the fullest convictions that prayer is not only my duty—not only necessary as the appointed means of receiving those supplies, without which I can do nothing, but likewise the greatest honour and privilege to which I can be admitted in the present life,—I should still find myself so unwilling to engage in it. It seems that if I durst, or could do altogether without it, I should be willing. However, I think it is not prayer itself that I am weary of, but such prayers as mine. How can it be accounted prayer, when the heart is so little affected,—when it is polluted with such a mixture of vile and vain imaginations,—when I hardly know what I say myself,—but I feel my mind collected one minute, the next, my thoughts are gone to the ends of the earth. If what I express with my lips were written down, and the thoughts which at the same time are passing through my heart were likewise written between the lines, the whole taken together would be such an absurd and incoherent jumble—such a medley of inconsistence, that it might pass for the ravings of a lunatic. When [Satan] points out to me the wildness of this jargon, and asks, is this a prayer fit to be presented to the holy heart-searching God? I am at a loss what to answer, till it is given me to recollect that I am not under the law, but under grace,—that my hope is to be placed, not in my own prayers, but in the righteousness and intercession of Jesus. The poorer and viler I am in myself, so much the more is the power and riches of His grace magnified in my behalf. Therefore I must, and, the Lord being my helper, I will pray on, and admire his condescension and love, that He can and does take notice of such a creature,—for the event shows, that those prayers which are even displeasing to myself, partial as I am in my own case, are acceptable to Him, how else should they be answered? and that I am still permitted to come to a throne of grace,—still supported in my walk and in my work, and that mine enemies have not yet prevailed against me, and triumphed over me, affords a full proof that the Lord has heard and has accepted my poor prayers,—yea, it is possible, that those very prayers of ours of which we are most ashamed, are the most pleasing to the Lord, and for that reason, because we are ashamed of them. When we are favoured with what we call enlargement, we come away tolerably satisfied with ourselves, and think we have done well.

NOTES

1. Fanny Crosby—Fanny Crosby, "Come in our midst, O gracious Lord," Hymnary.org, https://hymnary.org/text/come_in_our_midst_o_gracious_lord.

2. Prayer of Jabez—1 Chronicles 4:10.

3. Thomas à Kempis—Thomas à Kempis, *The Imitation of Christ*, Christian Classics Ethereal Library, https://ccel.org/ccel/kempis/imitation/imitation .THREE.21.html.

4. George Webb—"Short direction for the daily exercise of the Christian," London 1625, courtesy of Plimoth Plantation, quoted in Peggy M. Baker, "Giving Thanks: The Religious Roots of Thanksgiving," November–December 2001, Pilgrim Hall Museum, https://www.pilgrimhall.org/giving_thanks.htm.

5. Francis Paget—"Francis Paget (1851–1911)," St. Matthew's Westminster, https://www.stmw.org/paget.html.

6. Queen Lili`uokalani—Queen Lili`uokalani, "Queen's Prayer (Ke Aloha O Ka Haku)," March 22, 1895, https://www.kalena.com/huapala/Q/Queens _Prayer.html.

7. Prayer of St. Francis of Assisi—"The St. Francis Prayer—Make Me an Instrument of Your Peace," March 10, 2021, Crosswalk.com, https://www .crosswalk.com/faith/prayer/the-prayer-of-st-francis-make-me-an-instrument .html.

8. William Wilberforce—Trevin Wax, "I Know Not What I Am, But to You I Flee: A Prayer of William Wilberforce," September 1, 2013, The Gospel Coalition, https://www.thegospelcoalition.org/blogs/trevin-wax/i-know-not -what-i-am-but-to-you-i-flee-a-prayer-of-william-wilberforce/.

9. Thomas Dorsey—Thomas A. Dorsey, "Precious Lord, Take My Hand," https://www.austincc.edu/dlauderb/2341/Lyrics/PreciousLord.htm.

10. Jonah—Jonah 2:2–9.

11. St. Teresa of Ávila—Gretchen Filz, "Read St. Teresa of Avila's Famous Poem, in Her Own Handwriting," October 16, 2015, *Catholic Company*

Magazine, https://www.catholiccompany.com/magazine/nada-te-turbe-teresa-avila-poem-5760.

12. The O Antiphons of Advent—"The 'O Antiphons' of Advent," United States Conference of Catholic Bishops, https://www.usccb.org/prayer-and-worship/prayers-and-devotions/prayers/the-o-antiphons-of-advent.

13. Bishop Charles H. Mason—James Melvin Washington, "Charles Harrison Mason," in *Conversations with God: Two Centuries of Prayers by African Americans* (New York: HarperCollins, 1994), 114.

14. Charles Vaughan—Dorothy M. Stewart, comp., *The Westminster Collection of Christian Prayers* (Louisville: Westminster John Knox Press, 1999), 92, https://www.google.com/books/edition/The_Westminster_Collection_of_Christian/kfvh5CkU6-AC.

15. Naval Prayer—Emily Sears, "May the Vessels of Our Navy Be Guarded," July 23, 2012, http://caseforprayer.com/may-the-vessels-of-our-navy-be-guarded/.

16. Gloria—"Gloria," Marquette University, https://www.marquette.edu/faith/prayers-gloria.php.

17. Magnificat—The Prayer of Mary—"The Magnificat: The Prayer of Mary," Eternal Word Television Network, https://www.ewtn.com/catholicism/devotions/magnificat-392.

18. Blaise Pascal—"Pascal's Memorial," Christian Classics Ethereal Library, https://ccel.org/ccel/pascal/memorial/memorial.i.html.

19. Søren Kierkegaard—"The Prayers of Soren Kierkegaard: Nine Prayers That Reveal Kierkegaard's Spiritual Longing," The Words Group, http://www.thewords.com/articles/soren1.htm.

20. George Herbert—George Herbert, "Mattens," *The Temple*, Christian Classics Ethereal Library, https://www.ccel.org/h/herbert/temple/Mattens.html.

21. Hannah—1 Samuel 2:1–10 ESV.

22. St. Elizabeth Ann Seton—Mark Pasko, "23. Healing and Preaching (Lord, Increase My Faith)," *Devotions: Saints*, Christian Classics Ethereal Library, https://ccel.org/ccel/pasko/saints/saints.ii_1.html.

23. Thomas More—"Prayers by Thomas More," Center for Thomas More Studies, Thomas More College of Liberal Arts, https://thomasmorecollege.edu/2019/04/prayers-by-thomas-more/.

24. St. Francis of Assisi—Regis J. Armstrong, J. A. Wayne Hellmann, and William J. Short, *Francis of Assisi—The Saint: Early Documents*, Vol. 1 (New York: New City Press, 1999), 161, https://books.google.com/books/about/Francis_of_Assisi_The_Saint_Early_Docume.html?id=vwVsEM8mXWYC.

25. Thomas Traherne—"A Serious and Pathetical Contemplation of the Mercies of God," *Poetry Foundation*, https://www.poetryfoundation.org/poems/45416/a-serious-and-pathetical-contemplation-of-the-mercies-of-god.

26. Timothy Dwight—Timothy Dwight, "Lord of all worlds, incline Thy bounteous ear," Hymnary.org, https://hymnary.org/text/lord_of_all_worlds_incline_thy_bounteous.

27. Dwight L. Moody—D. L. Moody, L. D. Sankey, et al., *"The Gospel Awakening," Comprising the Sermons and Addresses, Prayer-Meeting Talks*

and Bible Readings of the Great Revival Meetings Conducted by Moody and Sankey, ed. L. T. Remlap (Chicago: Fairbanks and Palmer Publishing, 1885), 721, https://books.google.com/books/about/The_Gospel_Awakening.html?id =arIPAAAAIAAJ.

28. St. Anselm—"A Prayer by St. Anselm of Canterbury," Loyola Press, https://www.loyolapress.com/catholic-resources/liturgical-year/lent/online -prayers-and-retreats/a-prayer-by-st-anselm-of-canterbury/.

29. Henry Scougal—Henry Scougal, *The Works of the Rev. H. Scougal: Containing the Life of God in the Soul of Man; with Nine Other Discourses on Important Subjects* (Boston: Pierce and Williams, 1831), 74–75, https://books.google.com/books/about/The_Works_of_the_Rev_H_Scougal .html?id=CEQAAAAAYAAJ.

30. William Booth—William Booth, "Send the Fire," Hymnary.org, https:// hymnary.org/text/thou_christ_of_burning_cleansing_flame.

31. Billy Sunday—William T. Ellis, *"Billy" Sunday, the Man and His Message*, chap. xxii, Bible Study Tools, https://www.biblestudytools.com/classics /billy-sunday-the-man-and-his-message/chapter-xxii.html.

32. Fyodor Dostoevsky—Fyodor Dostoevsky, *The Brothers Karamazov*, Christian Classics Ethereal Library, https://www.ccel.org/d/dostoevsky /karamozov/htm/book06/chapter03.html.

33. Charles Spurgeon—Zack Bilbrey, "The Prayers of Charles Spurgeon Day 15," Helix Bible Church, April 8, 2020, http://helixchurch.org/the-prayers -of-charles-spurgeon-day-15/.

34. Sojourner Truth—Sojourner Truth, "Isabella's Religious Experience," from *The Narrative of Sojourner Truth*, Page by Page Books, https://www .pagebypagebooks.com/Sojourner_Truth/The_Narrative_of_Sojourner_Truth /Isabellas_Religious_Experience_p6.html.

35. Harriet Tubman—Jean M. Humez, *Harriet Tubman: The Life and the Life Stories* (Madison: University of Wisconsin Press, 2003), 213, https://www .google.com/books/edition/Harriet_Tubman/k9l_lA3Inw4C?hl=en&gbpv=1& dq=tubman+%E2%80%9COh+Lord,+convert+master.+Oh+Lord,+change +that+man%E2%80%99s+heart!%E2%80%9D.+.+.+.&pg=PA213&printsec =frontcover.

36. Frederick Douglass—Frederick Douglass, *Life of an American Slave* (Boston: Anti-Slavery Office, 1845), 119, http://utc.iath.virginia.edu/abolitn /abaufda14t.html.

37. Amanda Berry Smith—Amanda Berry Smith, *An Autobiography, the Story of the Lord's Dealings with Mrs. Amanda Smith, the Colored Evangelist* (Chicago: Meyer & Brother, 1893), 184, https://www.google.com/books/edition/An _Autobiography_the_Story_of_the_Lord_s/WClaAAAAMAAJ?hl=en&gbpv =1&dq=%E2%80%9C%E2%80%98Help+me+to+throw+off+that+mean +feeling,+and+give+me+grace+to+be+a+gazing+stock.%E2%80%9D +amanda+smith&pg=PA184&printsec=frontcover.

38. W. E. B. Du Bois—W. E. Burghardt Du Bois, "A Litany of Atlanta," *The Book of American Negro Poetry*, ed. James Weldon Johnson (New York: Harcourt, Brace and Company, 1922), https://www.bartleby.com/269/26.html.

39. Maria W. Stewart—Maria W. Stewart, Prayer from "Meditation XII," *Meditations from the Pen of Mrs. Maria W. Stewart* . . . (Washington: Enterprise Publishing Company, 1879), https://digital.library.upenn.edu/women/stewart-maria/meditations/meditations.html.

40. Abraham Lincoln—Abraham Lincoln, "Second Inaugural Address," March 4, 1865, Washington, D.C., http://www.abrahamlincolnonline.org/lincoln/speeches/inaug2.htm.

41. George Washington—George Washington, "Circular to the States: George Washington to the States, June 8, 1783," https://www.mountvernon.org/education/primary-sources-2/article/circular-to-the-states-george-washington-to-the-states-june-8-1783/.

42. Ronald Reagan—Ronald Reagan, "Proclamation 5767—National Day of Prayer, 1988," February 3, 1988, Ronald Reagan Presidential Library and Museum, https://www.reaganlibrary.gov/archives/speech/proclamation-5767-national-day-prayer-1988.

43. John Jay—John Jay and William Jay, *The Life of John Jay: With Selections from His Correspondence and Miscellaneous Papers* (New York: J & J Harper, 1833), 518, https://www.google.com/books/edition/The_Life_of_John_Jay_The_life_of_John_Ja/k50EAAAAYAAJ?hl=en&gbpv=1&dq=thank+thee,+the+great+Sovereign+of+the+universe,+for+thy+long-continued+goodness+to+these+countries+-+jay&pg=PA518&printsec=frontcover.

44. John Adams—John Adams, "Letter from John Adams to Abigail Adams, 2 November 1800," Adams Family Papers, https://www.masshist.org/digitaladams/archive/doc?id=L18001102ja.

45. James Madison—James Madison, "Presidential Proclamation, [23 July] 1813," Founders Online, https://founders.archives.gov/documents/Madison/03-06-02-0434.

46. Franklin Delano Roosevelt—Franklin D. Roosevelt, "Franklin Roosevelt's D-Day Prayer," June 6, 1944, Our Documents: D-Day, http://docs.fdrlibrary.marist.edu/odddayp.html.

47. Jacob Duché—Jacob Duché, "First Prayer of the Continental Congress, 1774," September 7, 1774, Office of the Chaplain, https://chaplain.house.gov/archive/continental.html.

48. William Penn—William Penn, "William Penn's Prayer for Philadelphia, 1684," http://explorepahistory.com/odocument.php?docId=1-4-F.

49. Absalom Jones—Absalom Jones, "A Thanksgiving Sermon, preached January 1, 1808, in St. Thomas's, or the African Episcopal Church, Philadelphia" (Philadelphia: Fry and Kammerer, 1808), http://anglicanhistory.org/usa/ajones/thanksgiving1808.html.

50. William Tyndale—"William Tyndale—Lord, Open the King of England's Eyes," The Church of England (Continuing), https://cofec.org/resources/reformers/william-tyndale-lord-open-the-king-of-englands-eyes/.

51. Ludwig van Beethoven—Frances M. Young, *Can These Dry Bones Live?* (Eugene, OR: Wipf & Stock, 2010), 86, https://books.google.com/books?id=5ctMAwAAQBAJ&source=gbs_book_other_versions.

52. Clara Ann Thompson—Clara Ann Thompson, "Out of the Deep," Poetry Nook, https://www.poetrynook.com/poem/out-deep-0.

53. Richard Allen—Washington, James Melvin. *Conversations with God: Two Centuries of Prayers by African Americans* (New York: HarperCollins Publishers, 1994), 10, quoted in Bernice Johnson Reagon, lectionary, February 22, 2009, http://www.theafricanamericanlectionary.org/PopupCulturalAid.asp?LRID=70.

54. Benjamin Tucker Tanner—William Seraile, *Fire in His Heart: Bishop Benjamin Tucker Tanner and the A.M.E. Church* (Knoxville: University of Tennessee Press, 1998), 140, https://www.google.com/books/edition/Fire_in_His_Heart/O2RKOfJF2Q8C?hl=en&gbpv=1&dq=To+Thee,+oh+Lord,+we+make+our+plea+That+human+sorrows+Thou+wouldst+see,+And+human+grief%3B+and+human+tears+That+flow+throughout+the+life-long+years.+Awake,+O+Lord,+and+speak+the+word,&pg=PA140&printsec=frontcover.

55. Josephine D. Heard—Josephine D. Henderson Heard, "Unuttered Prayer," Poetry Nook, https://www.poetrynook.com/poem/unuttered-prayer.

56. Book of Common Prayer—Funeral Prayer—"The Committal," The (Online) Book of Common Prayer, Pastoral Offices, The Burial of the Dead: Rite Two, 501, https://www.bcponline.org/.

57. Apostles' Creed—"The Apostles' Creed: Traditional version," Reformed Church in America, https://www.rca.org/about/theology/creeds-and-confessions/the-apostles-creed/.

58. Andrew Murray—Andrew Murray, *With Christ in the School of Prayer*, Christian Classics Ethereal Library, https://www.ccel.org/ccel/murray/prayer.III.html.

59. John Calvin—John Calvin, *Tracts and Letters*, Volume 2, quoted in Doctrine and Devotion (podcast), http://www.doctrineanddevotion.com/podcast/back-to-school.

60. George Whitefield—Arnold A. Dallimore, *George Whitefield, the Life and Times of the Great Evangelist of the Eighteenth-century Revival* (Westchester, IL: Cornerstone Books, 1979), 16, https://www.google.com/books/edition/George_Whitefield_the_Life_and_Times_of/sn_ZAAAAMAAJ?hl=en&gbpv=0.

61. John Chrysostom—*The Project Gutenberg EBook of Prayers of the Early Church*, produced by Stephen Hutcheson, Dave Morgan, and the Online Distributed Proofreading Team at http://www.pgdp.net, https://www.gutenberg.org/files/48247/48247-h/48247-h.htm.

62. St. Basil—"Prayers Ancient and Modern 02/24," February 24, 2016, Women of Christianity, http://womenofchristianity.com/prayers-ancient-and-modern-0224/.

63. Polycarp—Polycarp, "Epistle of Polycarp to the Philippians," *Ante-Nicene Fathers*, Vol. 1, translated by Alexander Roberts and James Donaldson, edited by Alexander Roberts, James Donaldson, and A. Cleveland Coxe (Buffalo, NY: Christian Literature Publishing Co., 1885), revised and edited by Keven Knight, New Advent, https://www.newadvent.org/fathers/0136.htm.

64. Hannah Whitall Smith—Hannah Smith, "Example of a Prayer of Consecration," Hannah Whitehall Smith's journal, May 31, 1869, from *The*

Christian's Secret of a Holy Life: The Unpublished Personal Writings of Hannah Whitall Smith (Oak Harbor: Logos Research Systems, 1997), https://www.cslewisinstitute.org/webfm_send/364.

65. St. Ignatius Loyola—St. Ignatius Loyola, Prayers of the Saints, St. Matthew's Westminster, https://www.stmw.org/ignatius.html.

66. Martin Luther—Martin Luther, "Luther's Evening Prayer," Beliefnet, https://www.beliefnet.com/prayers/protestant/bedtime/luthers-evening-prayer.aspx.

67. Anne Bradstreet—Anne Bradstreet, "In Thankful Acknowledgment for the Letters I Received from My Husband Out of England," *The Works of Anne Bradstreet*, ed. Jeannine Hensley (Cambridge, MA: Harvard University Press, 1967), 269, https://books.google.com/books?id=8xqU1NjzncwC&dq=%22O+thou+that+hear%E2%80%99st+the+prayers+of+thine%22&source=gbs_navlinks_s.

68. Prayers of Grace for Meals—Deacon Greg Kandra, "Bless us, O Lord: Praying Before Meals," The Word Among Us, https://wau.org/resources/article/re_bless_us_o_lord_praying_before_meals/ and "Meal Time Prayers," Immanuel Lutheran Church, https://www.immanuel.us/index.php?/mobile_site/detail/meal-time-prayers.

69. St. Richard of Chichester—St. Richard of Chichester, "Prayer of Saint Richard of Chichester," Loyola Press, https://www.loyolapress.com/catholic-resources/prayer/traditional-catholic-prayers/saints-prayers/day-by-day-prayer-of-saint-richard-of-chichester/.

70. John Greenleaf Whittier—John Greenleaf Whittier, "All things are thine; no gift have we," Hymnary.org, https://hymnary.org/text/all_things_are_thine_no_gift_have_we.

71. Paul Laurence Dunbar—Paul Laurence Dunbar, "A Thanksgiving Poem," *Oak and Ivy* (Dayton, OH: United Brethren Publishing House, 1893), 29, https://www.libraries.wright.edu/special/dunbar/explore/oak-ivy/331.

72. Anna Shipton—"Anna Shipton Quote," LibQuotes, https://libquotes.com/anna-shipton/quote/lbb7l9s.

73. Walter Rauschenbusch—Leon Stier, "839) Prayers by Walter Rauschenbusch (a)," July 29, 2015, EmailMeditations, https://emailmeditations.wordpress.com/2015/07/29/839-prayers-by-walter-rauschenbusch-a/.

74. Dismas the Good Thief—"Good Thief Prayer," Daily-Prayers.org, https://www.daily-prayers.org/angels-and-saints/prayer-to-st-dismas-the-good-thief/.

75. Johann Sebastian Bach—"Jesus, Help!" March 7, 2017, A Collection of Prayers, https://acollectionofprayers.com/tag/johann-sebastian-bach/.

76. Albrecht Dürer—Richard Viladesau, *The Triumph of the Cross: The Passion of Christ in Theology and the Arts, from the Renaissance to the Counter-Reformation* (New York: Oxford University Press, 2008), 285, https://books.google.com/books?id=3K_RKPz94nAC&pg=PA285&dq=%22O+God+in+heaven,+have+mercy+on+us%22#v=onepage&q=%22madness%22&f=false.

77. John Newton—Shane Lems, "A Contrite Heart (The Prayer of John Newton)," May 8, 2012, The Reformed Reader, https://reformedreader.wordpress.com/2012/05/08/a-contrite-heart-the-prayer-of-john-newton/.

78. John Knox—John Knox, *Select Practical Writings of John Knox* (Edinburgh: The Assembly's Committee, 1845), 57–59, https://books.google.com/books?id=maRPAAAAcAAJ&source=gbs_navlinks_s.

79. John Donne—John Donne, "Prayer: A Confession by John Donne," March 8, 2016, The Value of Sparrows, https://thevalueofsparrows.wordpress.com/2016/03/08/prayer-a-confession-by-john-dunne/.

80. St. Augustine—"St. Augustine: Act of Hope," Archdiocese of Saint Paul and Minneapolis, https://www.archspm.org/faith-and-discipleship/prayer/catholic-prayers/st-augustine-act-of-hope/.

81. Victor Hugo—Victor Hugo, *Les Misérables*, trans. Isabel F. Hapgood, 1887, The Literature Network, http://www.online-literature.com/victor_hugo/les_miserables/135/.

82. Charles D'Arcy—"IV. Intercessory Prayers: General Intercessions, 1056," http://assets.newscriptorium.com/collects-and-prayers/parishprs3.htm.

83. The Lord's Prayer—Matthew 6:9–13 KJV.

84. Jane Austen—"Another Day Now Gone: Jane Austen's Third Prayer," June 20, 2011, Jane Austen Centre, https://janeausten.co.uk/blogs/jane-miscellany/another-day-now-gone-jane-austens-third-prayer *and* Jane Austen, *Mansfield Park* (London: G. Routledge and Co., 1857), 56, https://books.google.com/books?id=87B7njEZCjUC&printsec=frontcover&source=gbs_ge_summary_r&cad=0#v=onepage&q&f=false.

85. Harriet Beecher Stowe—Harriet Beecher Stowe, "Abide in me, O Lord," Hymnary.org, https://hymnary.org/text/abide_in_me_o_lord_and_i_in_thee.

86. St. Thérèse of Lisieux—"A Morning Prayer Written by St. Therese," Eternal Word Television Network, https://www.ewtn.com/catholicism/devotions/morning-prayer-written-by-st-therese-838.

87. George MacDonald—George MacDonald, "The Hands of the Father," from *Unspoken Sermons*, 1867, The Literature Network, http://www.online-literature.com/george-macdonald/unspoken-sermons/9/.

88. St. Patrick—"The Prayer of Saint Patrick," May 31, 2020, Journey With Jesus, https://www.journeywithjesus.net/poemsandprayers/668-saint-patrick-prayer.

89. Susanna Wesley—"A Prayer of Susanna Wesley," Discipleship Ministries, The United Methodist Church, https://www.umcdiscipleship.org/book-of-worship/a-prayer-of-susanna-wesley.

90. Fred Rogers—Amy Hollingsworth, "Mister Rogers: A Presence Transformed by Prayer," November 8, 2019, FaithGateway, https://www.faithgateway.com/mister-rogers-prayer/.

91. George Müller—Dan Graves, "Even the Wind Obeyed," Christian History Institute, https://christianhistoryinstitute.org/magazine/article/even-the-wind-obeyed.

92. Julian of Norwich—Mary C. Earle, *Julian of Norwich: Selections from Revelations of Divine Love—Annotated & Explained* (Woodstock, VT: SkyLight Paths Publishing, 2013), 101, https://books.google.com/books?id=LTMNAgAAQBAJ&source=gbs_navlinks_s.

93. George H. W. Bush—"Inaugural Address of George Bush," Friday, January 20, 1989, Yale Law School Lillian Goldman Law Library, https://avalon.law.yale.edu/20th_century/bush.asp.

94. Helen Hunt Jackson—Helen Hunt Jackson, "A Last Prayer," Poeticous, https://www.poeticous.com/helen-hunt-jackson/a-last-prayer.

95. Clement of Rome—St. Clement of Rome, "Epistle to the Corinthians (Completed Text)," Eternal Word Television Network, https://www.ewtn.com/catholicism/library/epistle-to-the-corinthians-completed-text-9065.

96. Phillis Wheatley—Phillis Wheatley, "Prayer," *Complete Writings* (New York: Penguin Books, 2001), 96, https://books.google.com/books?id=8_Xvy DBsNSMC&source=gbs_navlinks_s.

97. Elizabeth Fry—Elizabeth Gurney Fry, *Memoir of the Life of Elizabeth Fry: With Extracts from Her Journal and Letters*, Vol. 1 (London: Charles Gilpin and John Hatchard, 1847), 283, https://books.google.com/books/about/Memoir_of_the_Life_of_Elizabeth_Fry.html?id=58pAAAAAIAAJ.

98. Jeremy Taylor—Jeremy Taylor, *Holy Living,* Christian Classics Ethereal Library, https://www.ccel.org/ccel/taylor/holy_living.

99. John Wesley—Steve Manskar, "The Wesley Covenant Prayer and the Baptismal Covenant," January 1, 2018, Discipleship Ministries, The United Methodist Church, https://www.umcdiscipleship.org/blog/the-wesley-covenant-prayer-and-the-baptismal-covenant.

100. Leo Tolstoy—Paula Marvelly, "Leo Tolstoy: The Three Hermits," September 16, 2016, The Culturium, https://www.theculturium.com/leo-tolstoy-the-three-hermits/.

Some Advice on Prayer

George Müller—George Müller, "How I Ascertain the Will of God," *Salvation*, Vol. 5 (New York: WM. Cowper Conant, 1903), 39, https://books.google.com/books?id=8G4aAQAAIAAJ&source=gbs_navlinks_s.

John Bunyan—"With What Attitude Should We Pray?" Question 39, The New City Catechism, The Gospel Coalition, https://www.thegospelcoalition.org/new-city-catechism/with-what-attitude-should-we-pray/.

John Newton—John Newton, *Twenty-Five Letters Hitherto Unpublished of the Rev. John Newton*, ed. Robert Jones (Edinburgh: J. Johnstone, 1840), 110–12, https://books.google.com/books?id=lL9jAAAAcAAJ&source=gbs_navlinks_s.